Corrective Reading
Thinking SRA Basics
Comprehension A

Workbook

Siegfried Engelmann
Phyllis Haddox
Susan Hanner

 **SRA**

Columbus, OH

SRAonline.com

Send all inquiries to this address:
SRA/McGraw-Hill
4400 Easton Commons
Columbus, OH 43219

ISBN: 978-0-07-611159-6
MHID: 0-07-611159-8

9 QDB 14 13 12

The McGraw·Hill Companies

A

① ② ③ ④ ⑤

B

① ② ③

C

① ② ③ ④

D

① ②

②

③

All _____. Fido _____. So, _____.

E

Lesson A   **1**

ERRORS

1	2	TOTAL

A

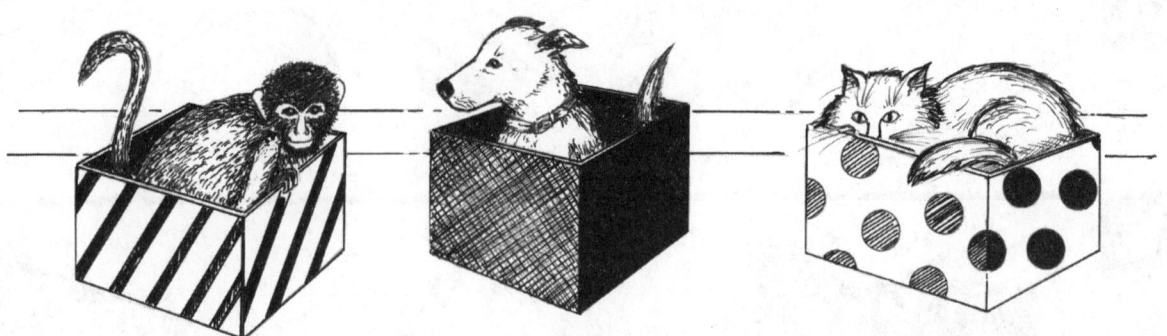

B

C

D

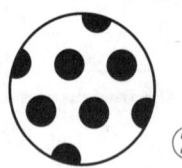
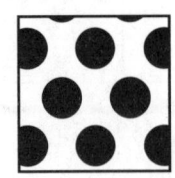

E

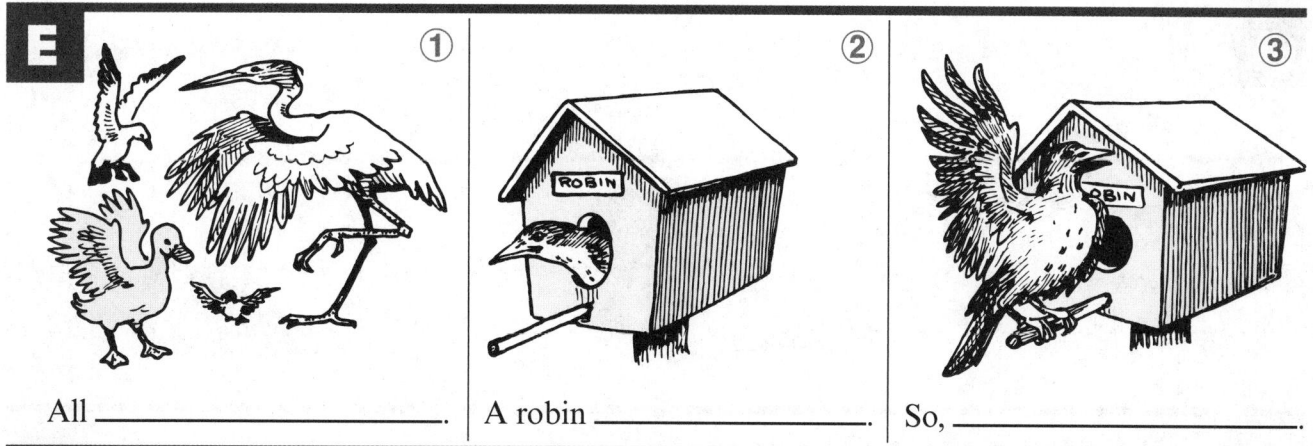

① ② ③

All _____.   A robin _____.   So, _____.

F

ERRORS			1	2	TOTAL

A

B

① ② ③ ④ ⑤

C

① ② ③ ④

D

① ② ③

All _____.

Tom _____.

So, _____.

E

F

① ② ③ ④ ⑤

ERRORS		1	2	TOTAL

A

B

C

D

All _____.

A trout _____.

So, _____.

E

F
① ② ③ ④ ⑤

G
① ② ③ ④ ⑤

H
① ② ③ ④ ⑤ ⑥

Lesson D   **7**

ERRORS

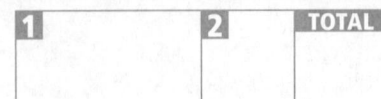

		1	2	TOTAL

A

B

C

①   ②   ③   ④

D

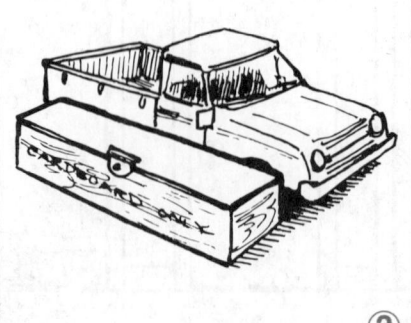

①   ②   ③

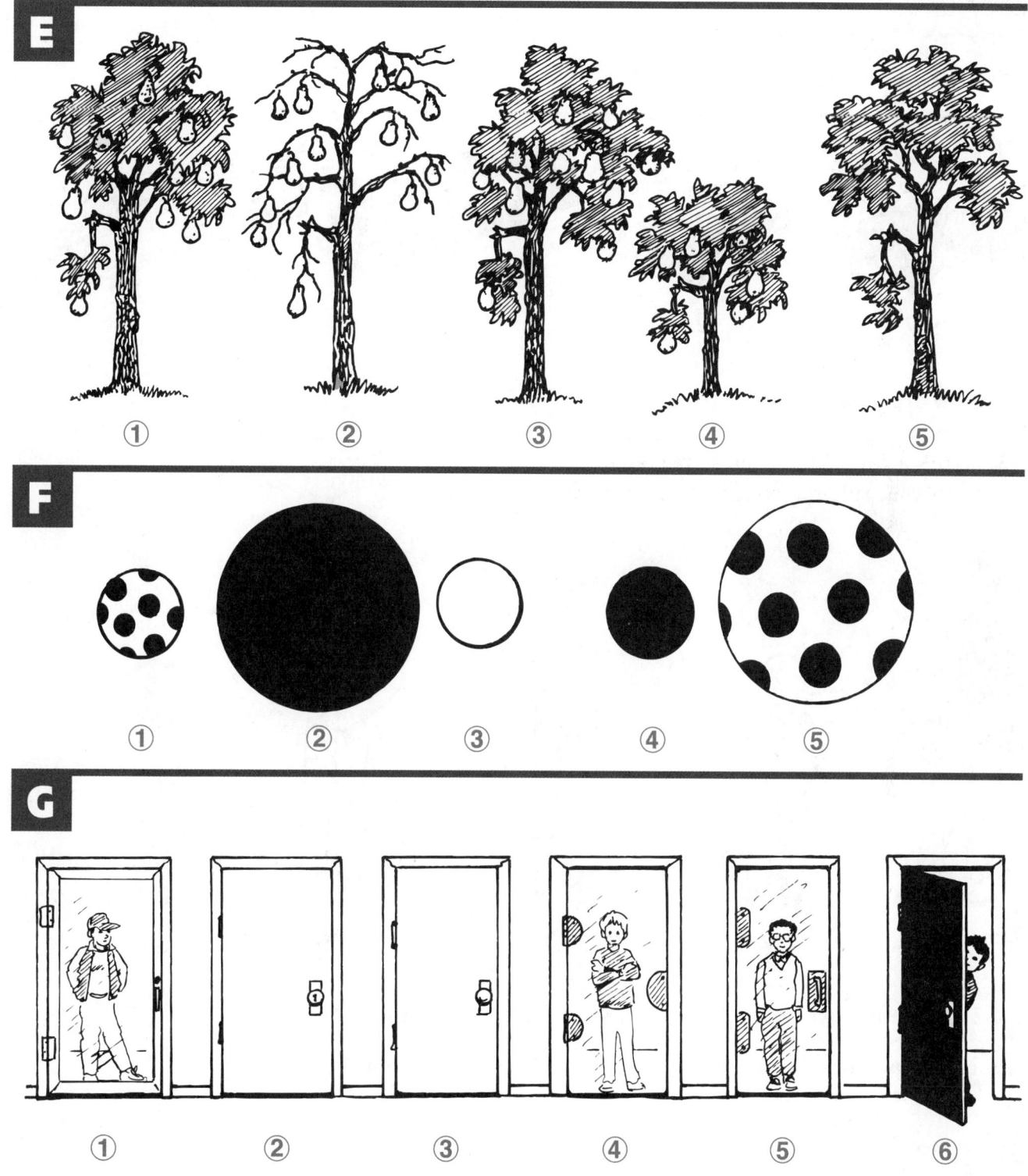

1	2	TOTAL

FACT GAME SCORECARD

1	2	3	4	5	6	7	8	9	10	11	12	13	14	15
16	17	18	19	20	21	22	23	24	25	26	27	28	29	30

1. How are vehicles 1 and 2 the same?

    ①   ②   ③   ④

2. How are objects 1 and 3 the same?

3. Here's a rule. **All the boys are standing.**
    Does that rule tell about all the pictures?

    ①   ②   ③   ④   ⑤

4. How many boys in the picture are sitting, **all, some,** or **none?**

5. How many boys in the picture are short, **all, some,** or **none?**

6. Here's a rule.

All the glass doors have a lion behind them.

Does that rule tell about object 1?

①   ②   ③

Lesson 1

ERRORS

1	2	3	4	TOTAL

A

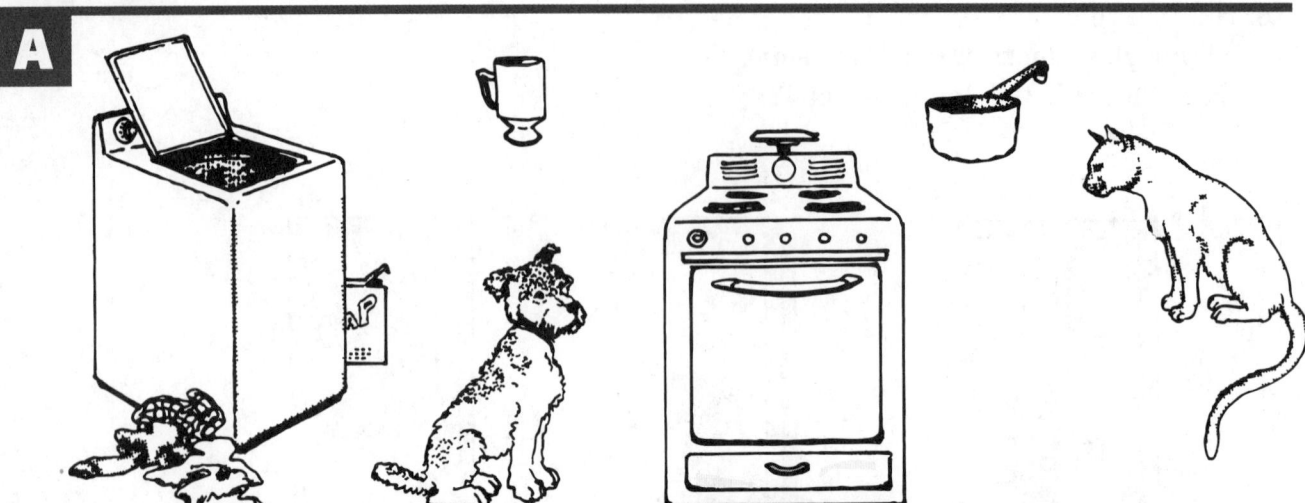

B

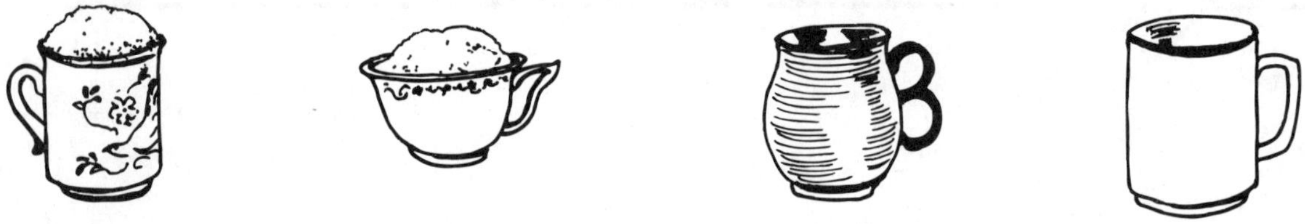

1. true false	**2.** true false	**3.** true false	**4.** true false

C

Circle the tools.
Make a line over the vehicles.

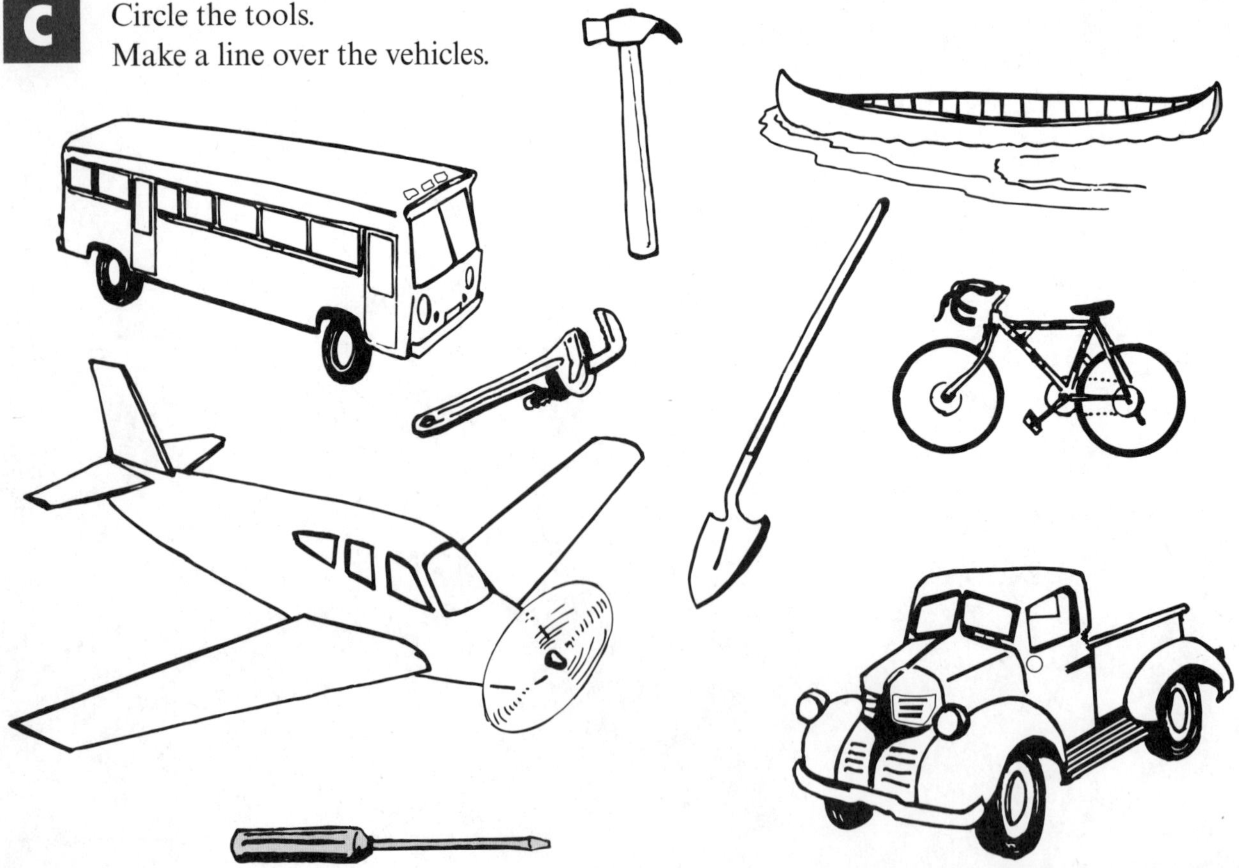

ERRORS | 1 | 2 | 3 | 4 | TOTAL

A

B

| **1.** true   false | **2.** true   false | **3.** true   false | **4.** true   false |

C

| **1.** true   false | **2.** true   false | **3.** true   false | **4.** true   false |

D Underline the containers.
Circle the animals.

Lesson 2   **13**

Lesson 3

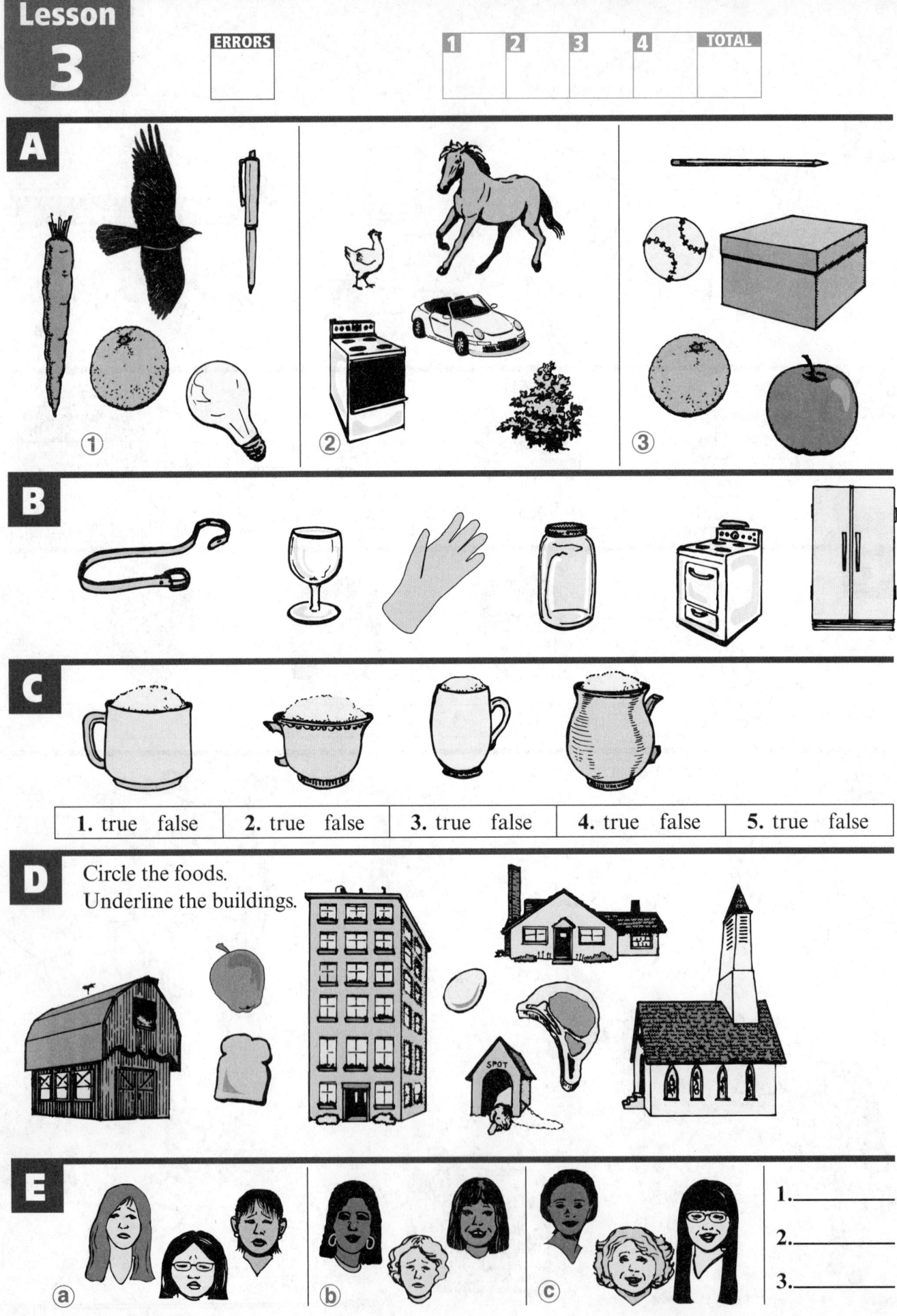

A

① ② ③

B

C

| **1.** true false | **2.** true false | **3.** true false | **4.** true false | **5.** true false |

D Circle the foods.
Underline the buildings.

SPOT

E

ⓐ ⓑ ⓒ

1._____
2._____
3._____

A

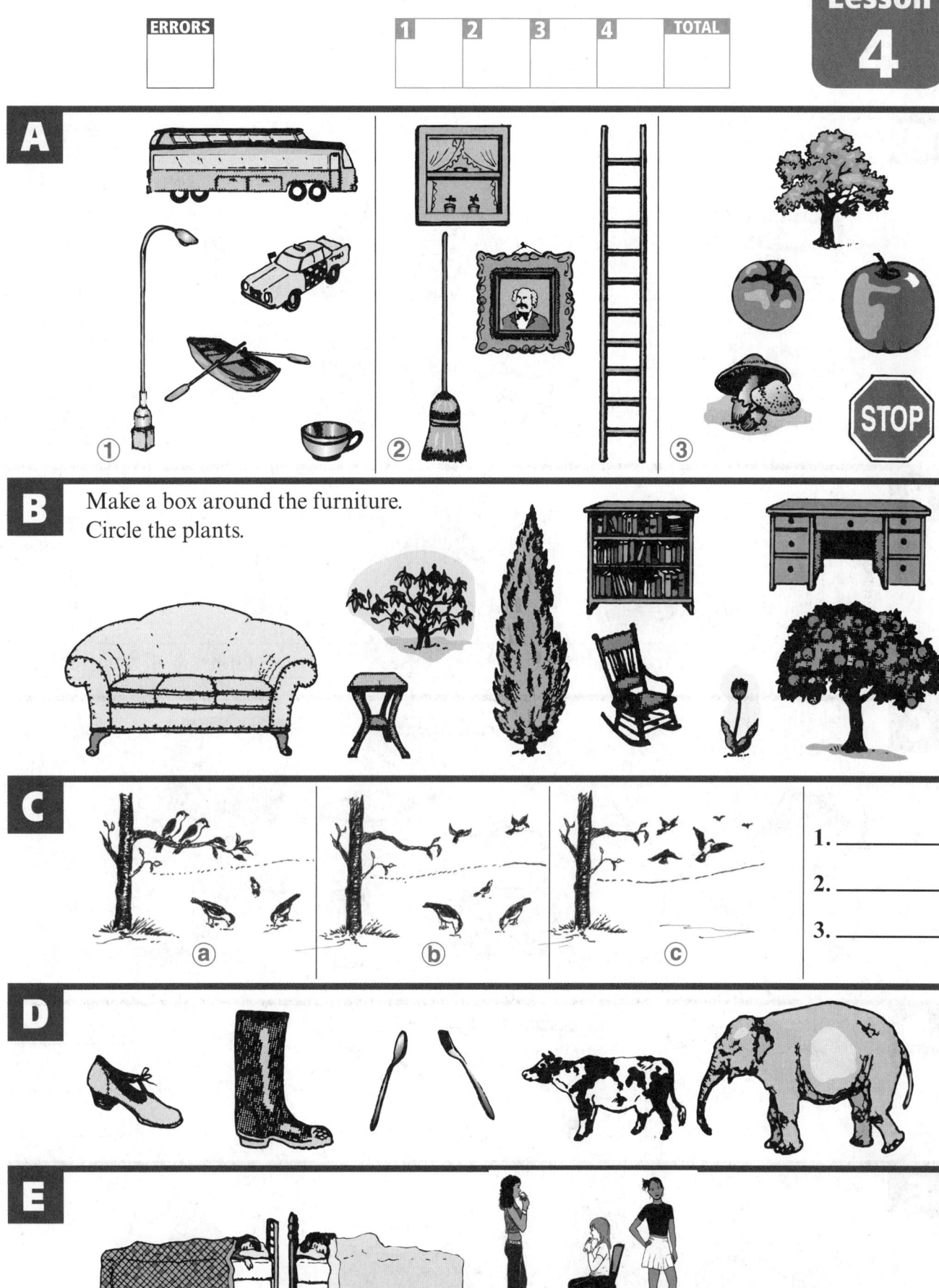

① ② ③

B Make a box around the furniture.
Circle the plants.

C

ⓐ ⓑ ⓒ

1. _____
2. _____
3. _____

D

E

| 1. true false | 2. true false | 3. true false | 4. true false |

ERRORS

1	2	3	4	TOTAL

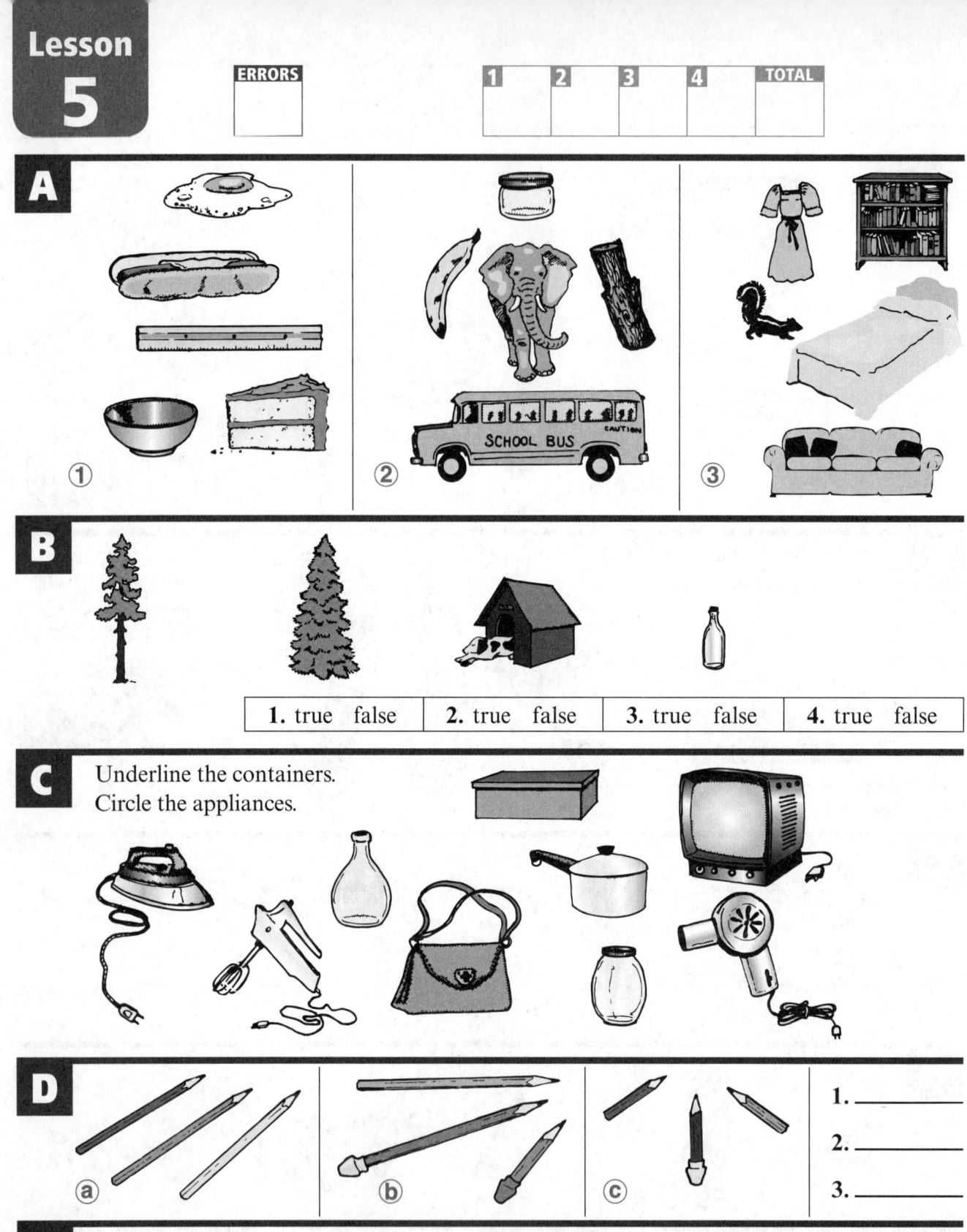

A

① ② ③

B

1. true false	**2.** true false	**3.** true false	**4.** true false

C Underline the containers.
Circle the appliances.

D

ⓐ ⓑ ⓒ

1. _____
2. _____
3. _____

E

1	2	3	4	5	6	7	8	9	10	11	12	13	14	15
16	17	18	19	20	21	22	23	24	25	26	27	28	29	30

ERRORS

1	2	TOTAL

1. How many months are in a year?

2. What does **obtain** mean?

3. Name the class these objects are in.
   Bus, boat, wagon, jet, bike.

4. How are a red house and a blue house the same?

5. How are a hammer and a saw the same?

6. All dogs bark. Collies are dogs.
   So, _____.

A Circle the containers.
   Make a line over the vehicles.

B

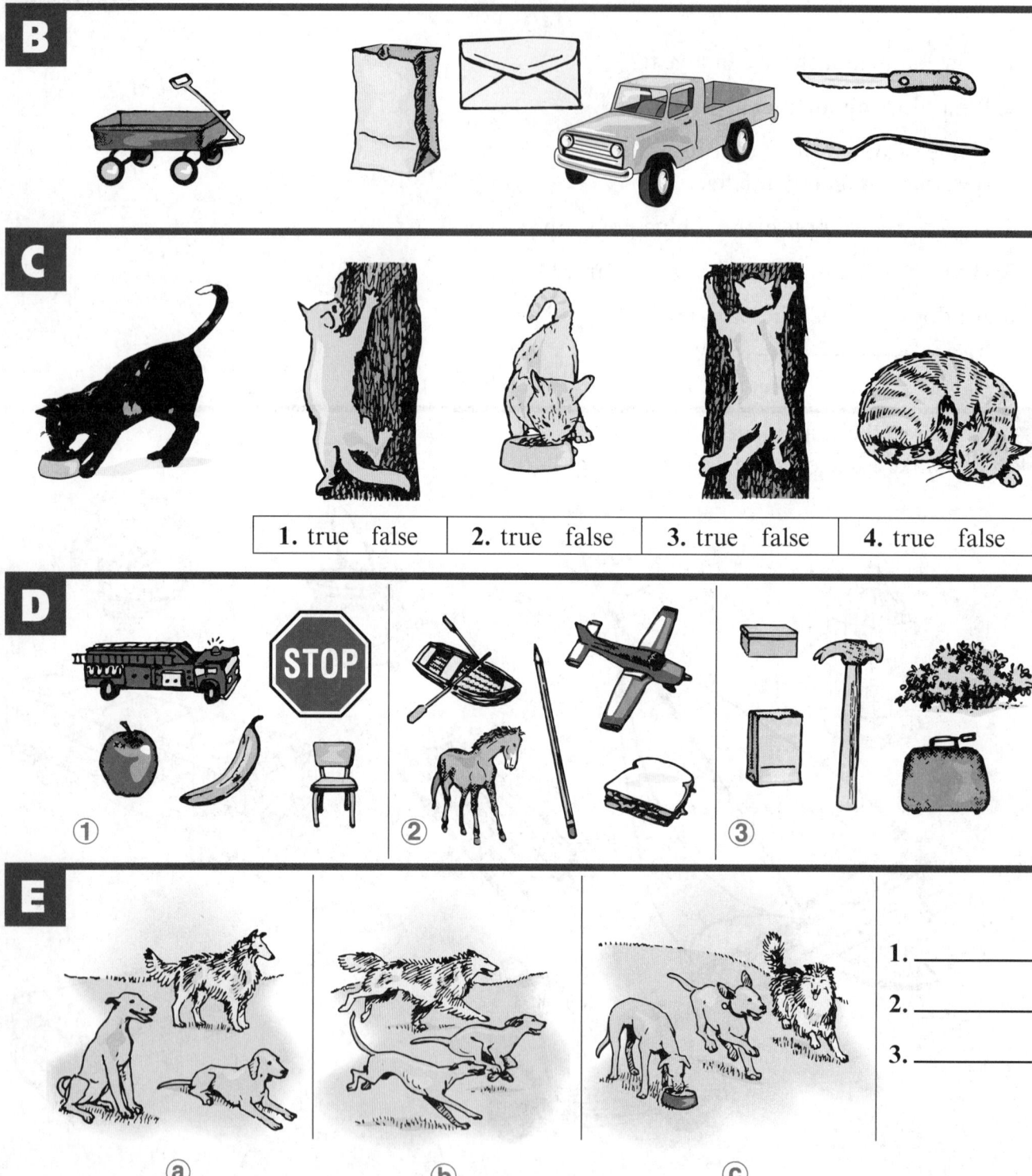

C

| **1.** true false | **2.** true false | **3.** true false | **4.** true false |

D

① ② ③

E

ⓐ ⓑ ⓒ

1. _____
2. _____
3. _____

ERRORS

	1	2	3	4	TOTAL

A

1. _____
2. _____
3. _____

B

1. _____
2. _____
3. _____

C

Circle the tools.
Underline the animals.

D

1. true false	**2.** true false	**3.** true false	**4.** true false

E

  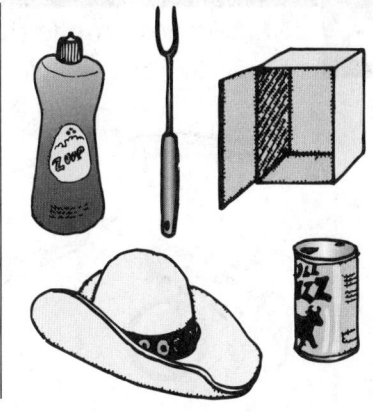

Lesson 6   **19**

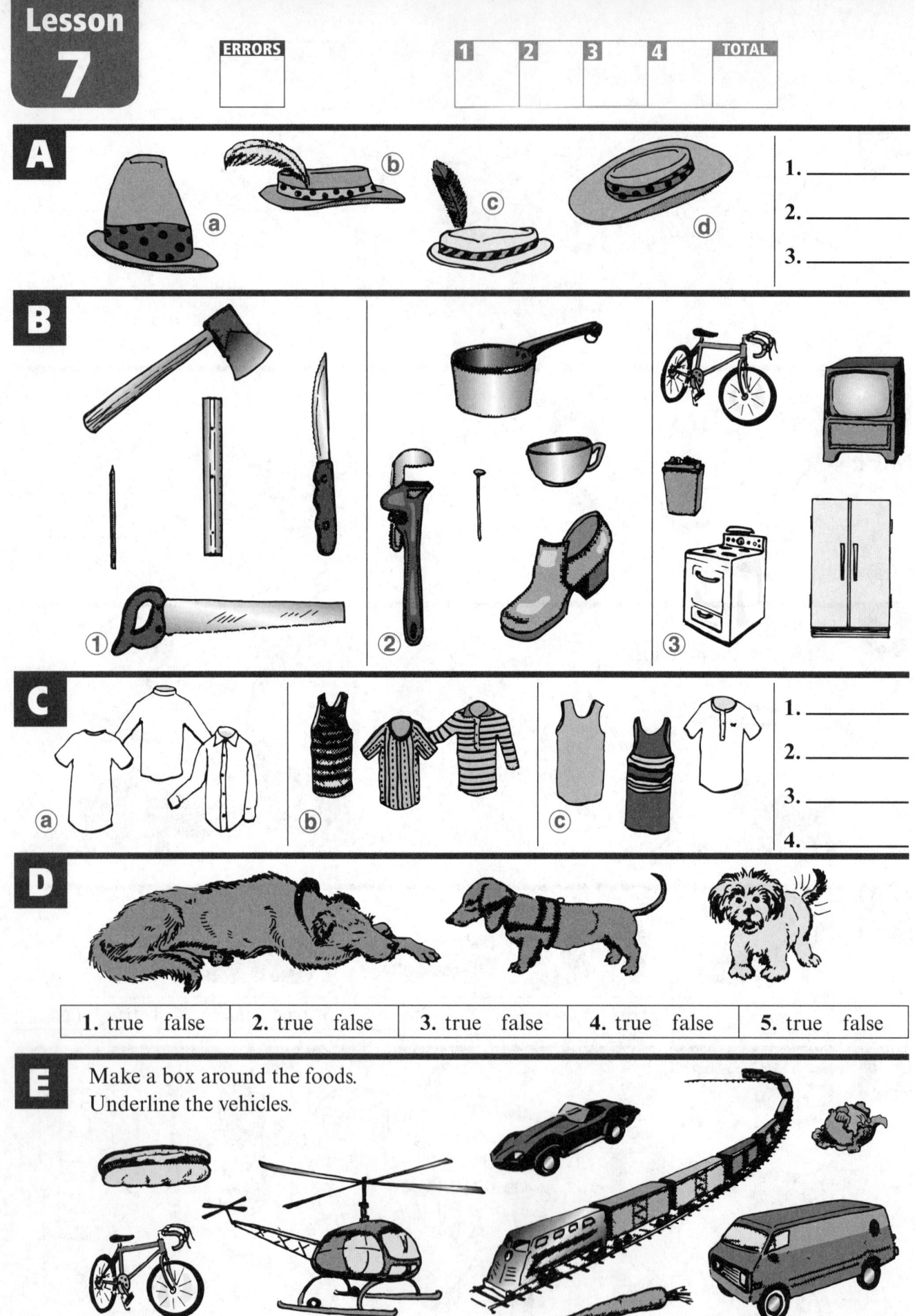

A

1. _____
2. _____
3. _____

B

① ② ③

C

1. _____
2. _____
3. _____
4. _____

ⓐ ⓑ ⓒ

D

1. true false	**2.** true false	**3.** true false	**4.** true false	**5.** true false

E Make a box around the foods.
Underline the vehicles.

ERRORS

1	2	3	4	TOTAL

A

① ② ③

B Make a box around the buildings.
Circle the furniture.

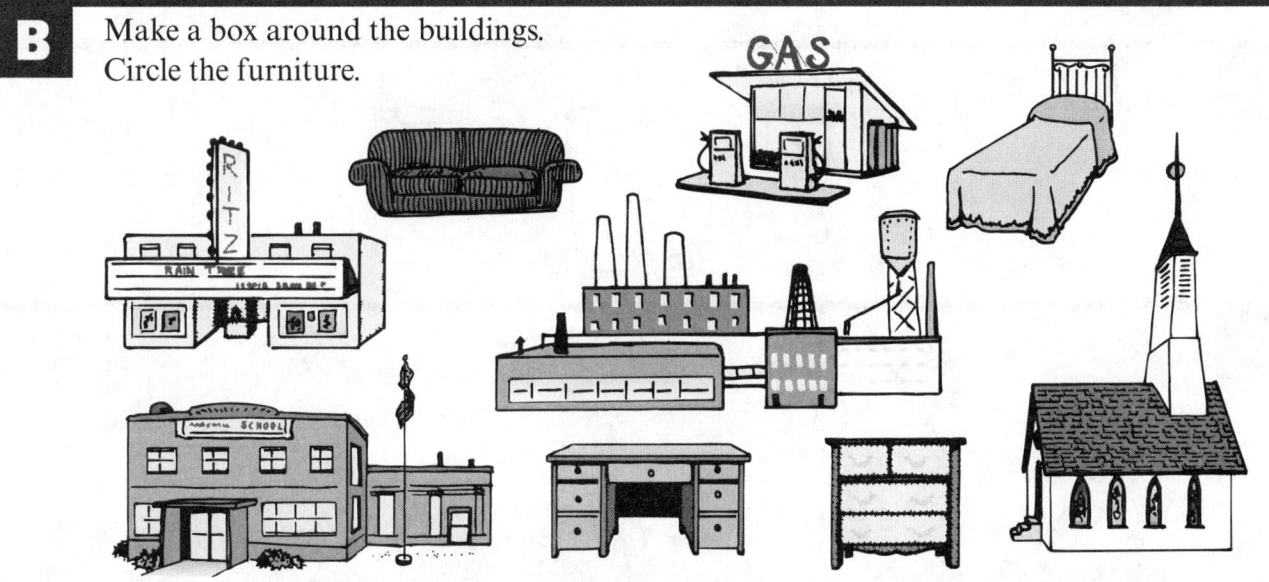

GAS

C

1. true false	**2.** true false	**3.** true false	**4.** true false	**5.** true false

D

ⓐ ⓑ ⓒ ⓓ

1. _____
2. _____
3. _____

ERRORS | 1 | 2 | 3 | 4 | TOTAL

A

Make a box around the plants.
Underline the appliances.

B

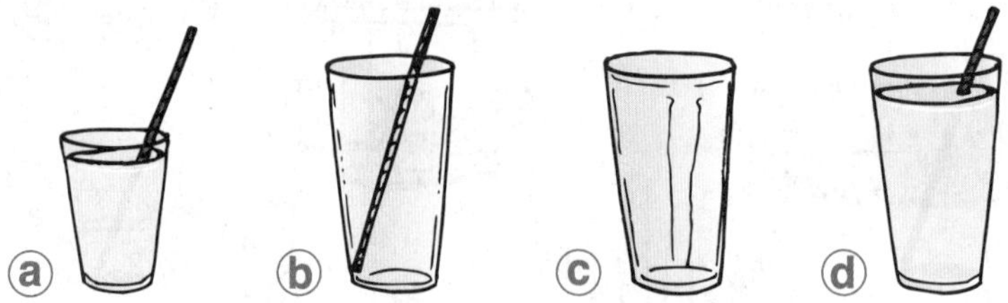

1. _____
2. _____
3. _____

C

① ② ③

D

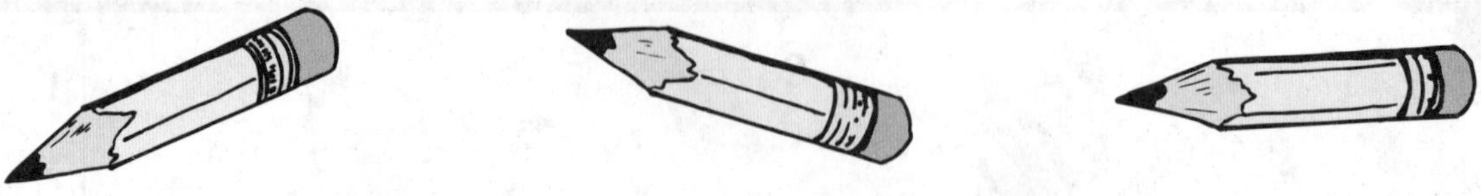

| 1. true false | 2. true false | 3. true false | 4. true false | 5. true false |

ERRORS		1	2	3	4	TOTAL

A

B

① ② ③

C

ⓐ ⓑ ⓒ

1. _____
2. _____
3. _____
4. _____

D Underline the vehicles.
Make a box around the tools.

E

1. true false	2. true false	3. true false	4. true false	5. true false

Lesson 11

	1	2	3	4	TOTAL

A

  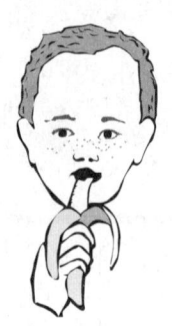

1. true   false   maybe
2. true   false   maybe
3. true   false   maybe
4. true   false   maybe
5. true   false   maybe

B

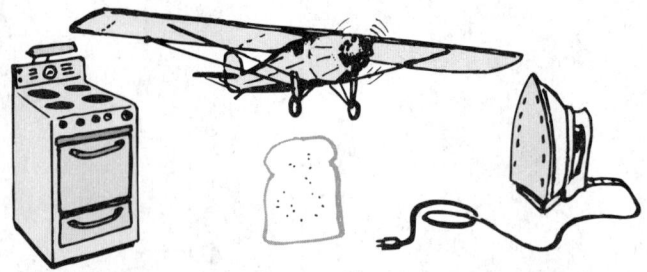 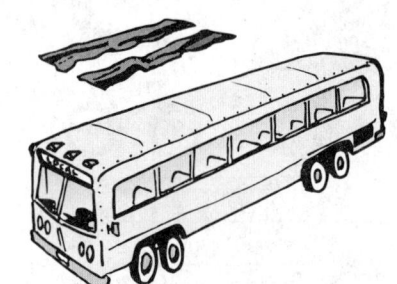

C

①

②

③

D

Circle the foods.
Make a box around the buildings.

ERRORS | 1 | 2 | 3 | 4 | TOTAL

A

1. true   false   maybe

2. true   false   maybe

3. true   false   maybe

4. true   false   maybe

B Underline the furniture.
Make a box around the containers.

C

 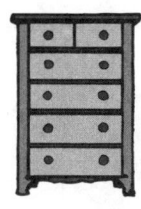
①

②

③

D

   ⓒ

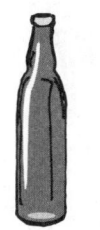 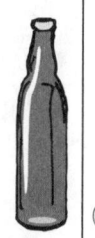 ⓓ

 ⓔ

1. _____

2. _____

3. _____

4. _____

E

 ⓐ

 ⓑ

 ⓒ

 ⓓ

1. _____

2. _____

3. _____

ERRORS

1	2	3	4	TOTAL

A Circle the plants.
Underline the foods.

B

1. true	false	maybe
2. true	false	maybe
3. true	false	maybe
4. true	false	maybe
5. true	false	maybe

C

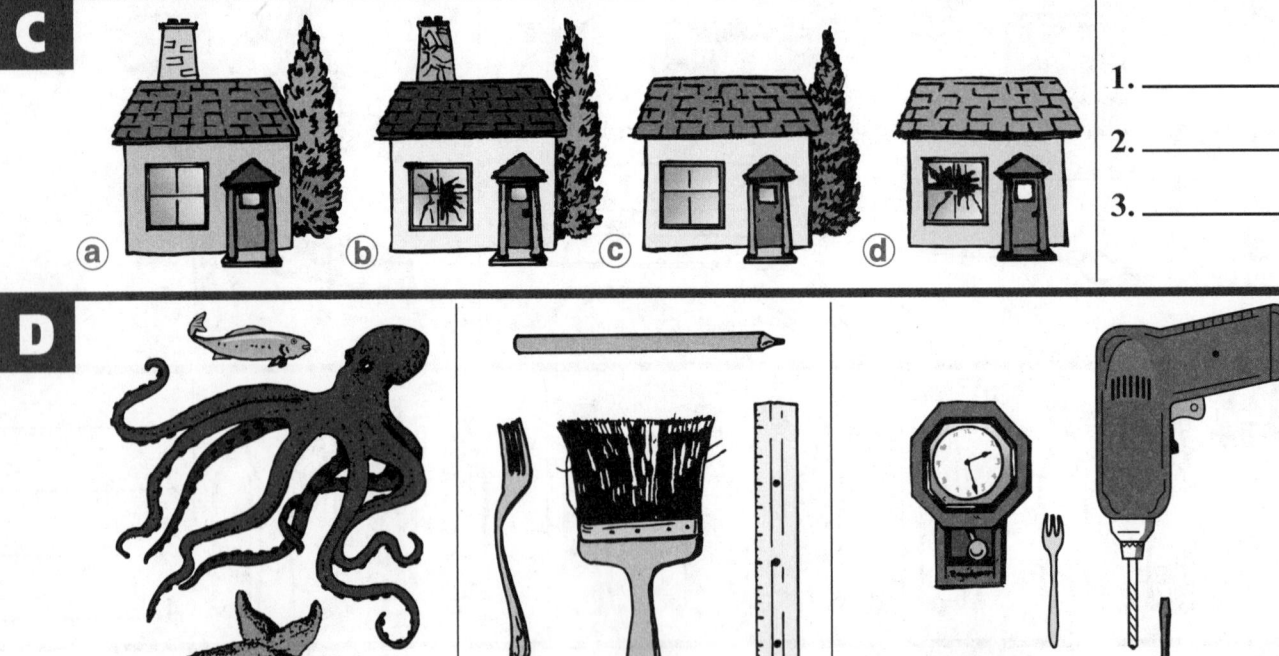

ⓐ   ⓑ   ⓒ   ⓓ

1. _____
2. _____
3. _____

D

① ② ③

ERRORS		1	2	3	4	TOTAL

A

    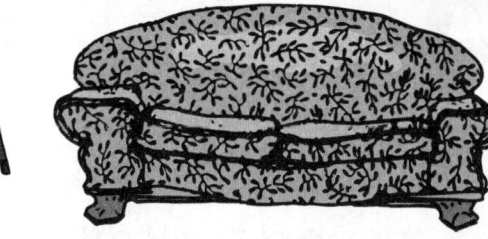

B

1. true	false	maybe
2. true	false	maybe
3. true	false	maybe
4. true	false	maybe

C

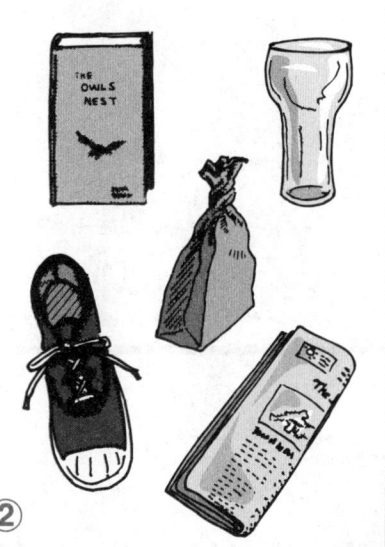

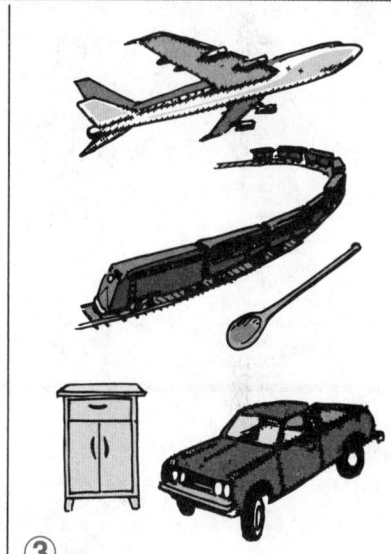

① ② ③

D

Circle the appliances.
Make a box around the vehicles.

    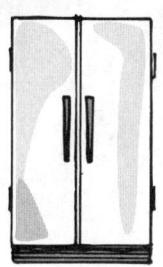

ERRORS

1	2	3	4	TOTAL

A Circle the furniture.
Underline the containers.

B

1. true   false   maybe

2. true   false   maybe

3. true   false   maybe

4. true   false   maybe

C

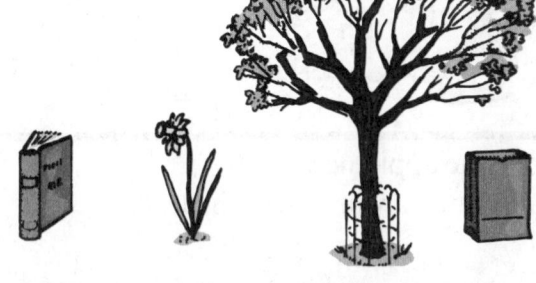

D

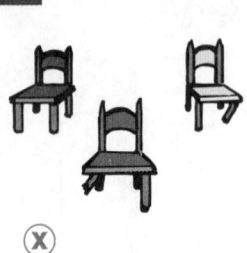
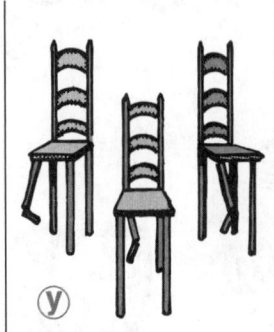
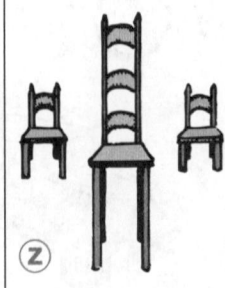

(x)   (y)   (z)

1. _____
2. _____
3. _____
4. _____

FACT GAME SCORECARD

1	2	3	4	5	6	7	8	9	10	11	12	13	14	15
16	17	18	19	20	21	22	23	24	25	26	27	28	29	30

ERRORS

1	2	3	TOTAL

1. What season comes after spring?

2. Name the seasons of the year.

3. What's a synonym for **indolent?**

4. Figure out the class of animals.
   These animals are cold-blooded and are born on land.

5. Snakes don't walk. Cobras are snakes.
   So, _____.

6. Here's a rule. **All boys eat.**
   Say the rule with **every.**

A

1. true   false   maybe

2. true   false   maybe

3. true   false   maybe

4. true   false   maybe

5. true   false   maybe

B   Circle the tools.
Underline the buildings.

Fact Game 3   **29**

C

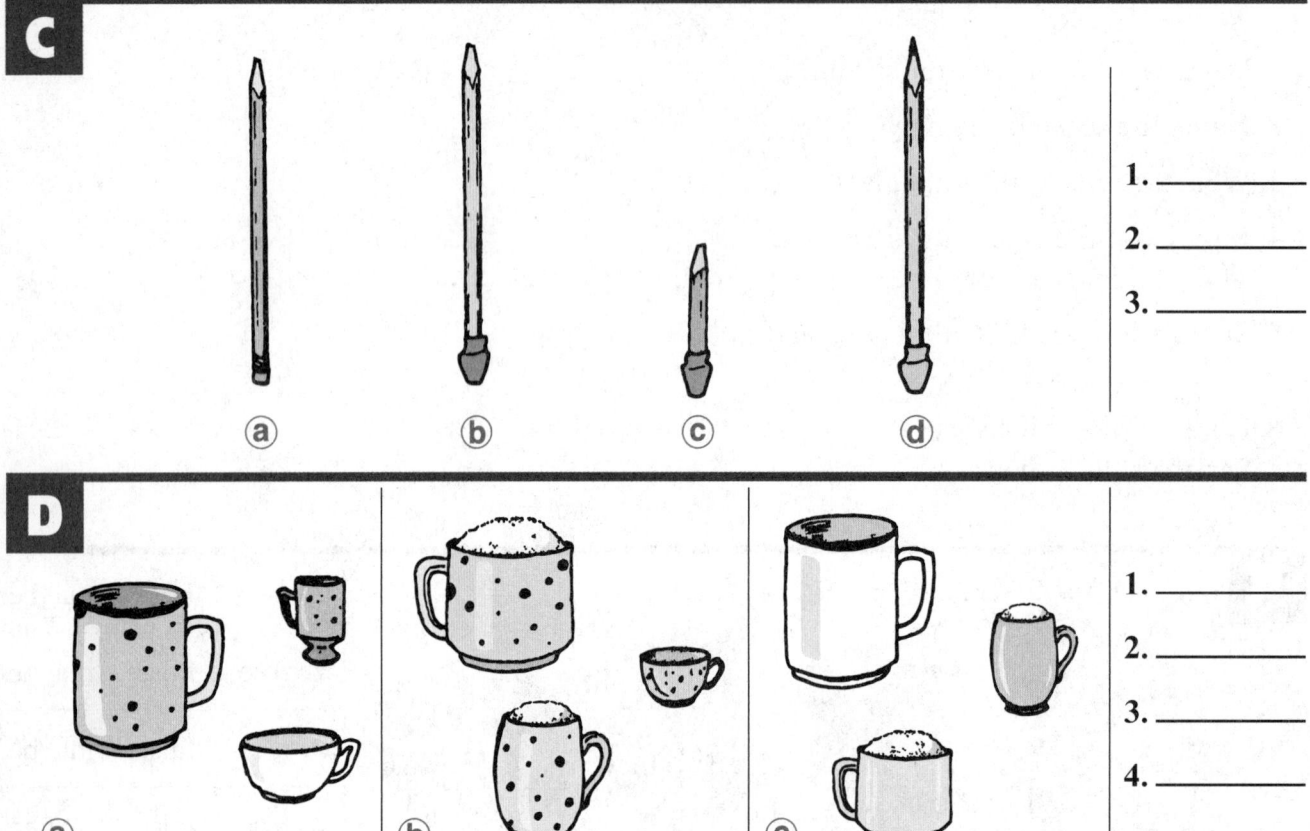

1. _____

2. _____

3. _____

D

1. _____

2. _____

3. _____

4. _____

A

 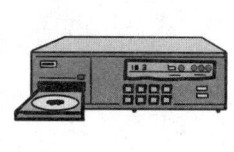   

B

  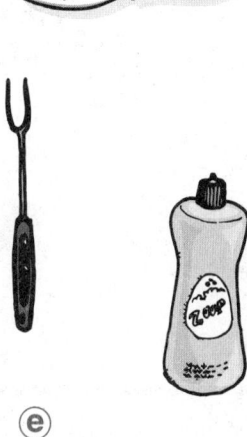

ⓒ ⓓ ⓔ

1. _____
2. _____
3. _____
4. _____

C

  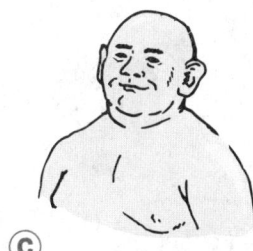 

ⓐ ⓑ ⓒ ⓓ

1. _____
2. _____
3. _____

D

1. true   false   maybe

2. true   false   maybe

3. true   false   maybe

4. true   false   maybe

ERRORS		1	2	3	4	TOTAL

A

1. true   false   maybe

2. true   false   maybe

3. true   false   maybe

4. true   false   maybe

B

 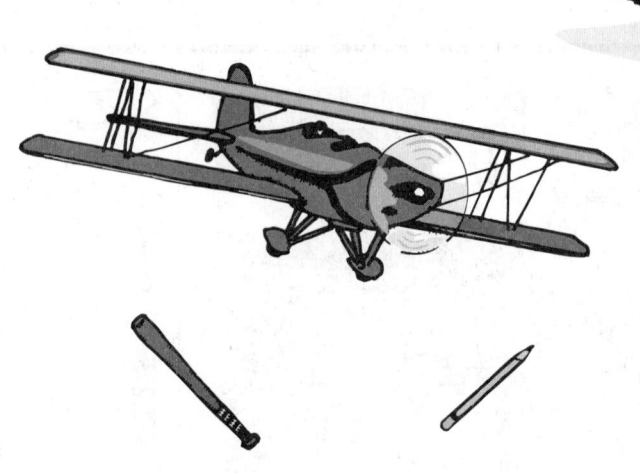 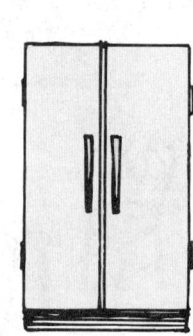

C

ⓜ   ⓝ   ⓞ

1. _____

2. _____

3. _____

4. _____

D

ⓐ   ⓑ   ⓒ   ⓓ

1. _____

2. _____

3. _____

ERRORS | 1 | 2 | 3 | 4 | **TOTAL**

A

B

   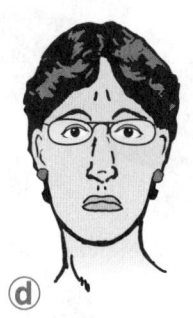

1. true   false   maybe

2. true   false   maybe

3. true   false   maybe

4. true   false   maybe

C

ⓐ   ⓑ   ⓒ   ⓓ

1. _____

2. _____

3. _____

D   Put an **A** on the vehicles.
Put a **B** on the tools.

ERRORS		1	2	3	4	TOTAL

A

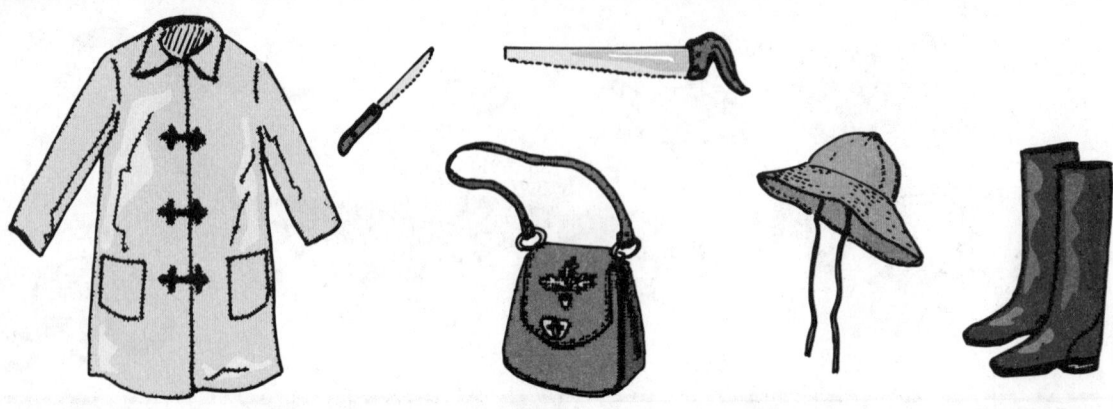

B

1. true   false   maybe

2. true   false   maybe

3. true   false   maybe

4. true   false   maybe

C

ⓐ ⓑ ⓒ ⓓ

1. _____
2. _____
3. _____

D

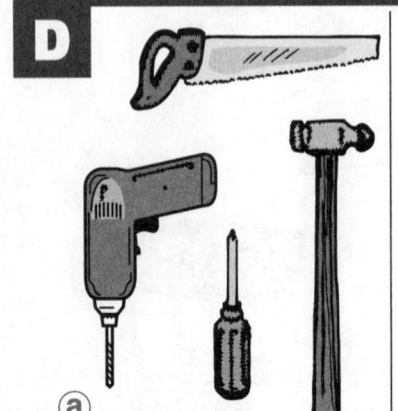  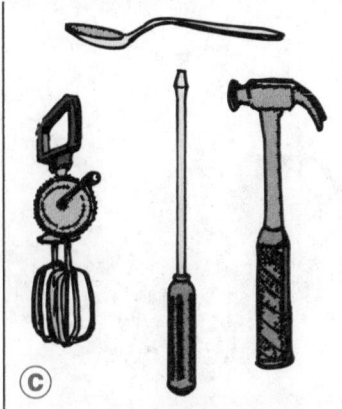

ⓐ ⓑ ⓒ

1. _____
2. _____
3. _____
4. _____

A

1. true	false	maybe
2. true	false	maybe
3. true	false	maybe
4. true	false	maybe

ERRORS

TOTAL

TEST 1

A

B

ⓐ   ⓑ   ⓒ

1. _____
2. _____
3. _____
4. _____

C

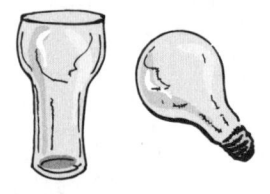

①

②

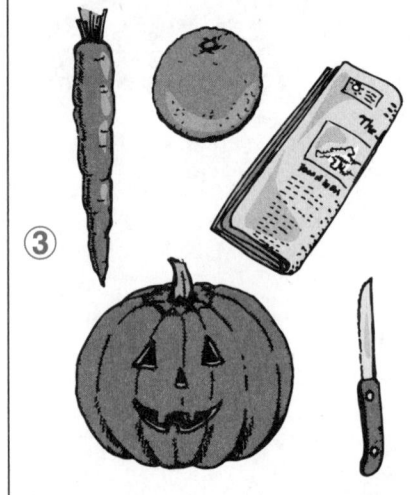

③

D

   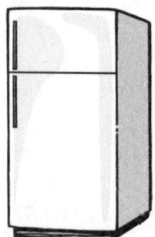

1. true	false	maybe	
2. true	false	maybe	
3. true	false	maybe	
4. true	false	maybe	

E

1. Pass   Fail   2. Pass   Fail

F

1. Pass   Fail

ERRORS | 1 | 2 | 3 | 4 | TOTAL

A

1. true false maybe
2. true false maybe
3. true false maybe
4. true false maybe

B

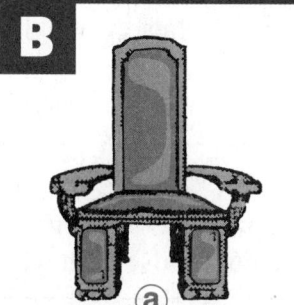 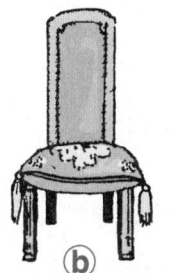  

ⓐ   ⓑ   ⓒ   ⓓ

1. _____
2. _____
3. _____

C

 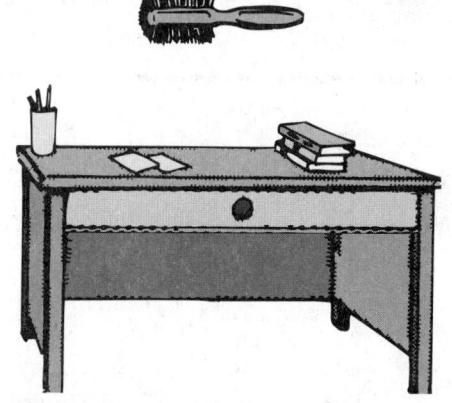

D

1. true false maybe
2. true false maybe
3. true false maybe
4. true false maybe
5. true false maybe
6. true false maybe

ERRORS | 1 | 2 | 3 | 4 | TOTAL

A

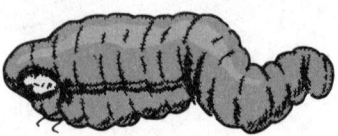

B

1. true false maybe
2. true false maybe
3. true false maybe
4. true false maybe
5. true false maybe
6. true false maybe

C

1. true false maybe	5. true false maybe
2. true false maybe	6. true false maybe
3. true false maybe	7. true false maybe
4. true false maybe	

D

1. _____
2. _____
3. _____
4. _____

ⓐ ⓑ ⓒ

ERRORS

	1	2	3	4	TOTAL

A

1.	true	false	maybe
2.	true	false	maybe
3.	true	false	maybe
4.	true	false	maybe
5.	true	false	maybe
6.	true	false	maybe

B

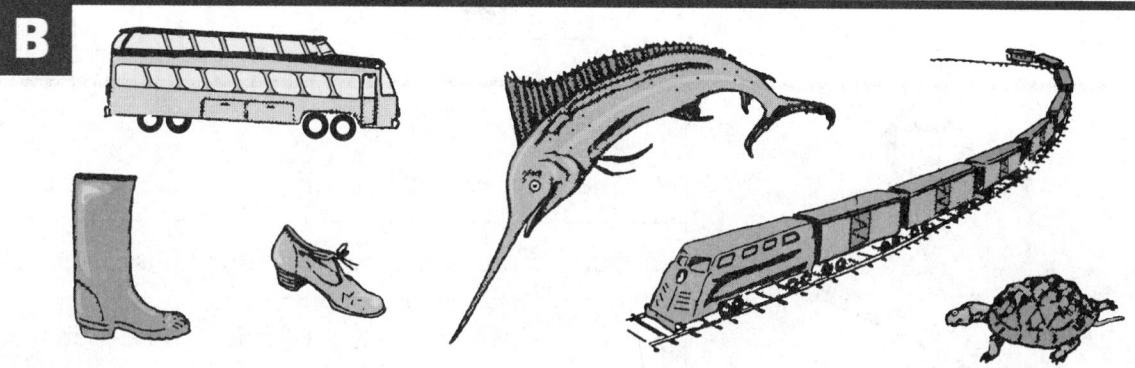

C

1.	true	false	maybe
2.	true	false	maybe
3.	true	false	maybe
4.	true	false	maybe
5.	true	false	maybe
6.	true	false	maybe

D

ⓐ　　　ⓑ　　　ⓒ　　　ⓓ

1. _____

2. _____

3. _____

A-1

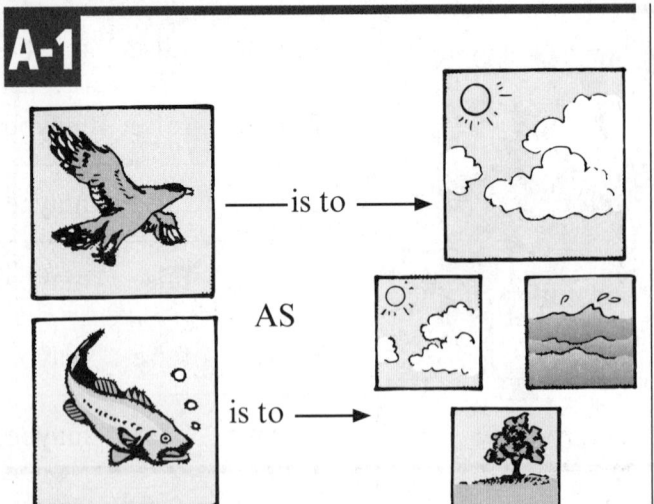

A-2

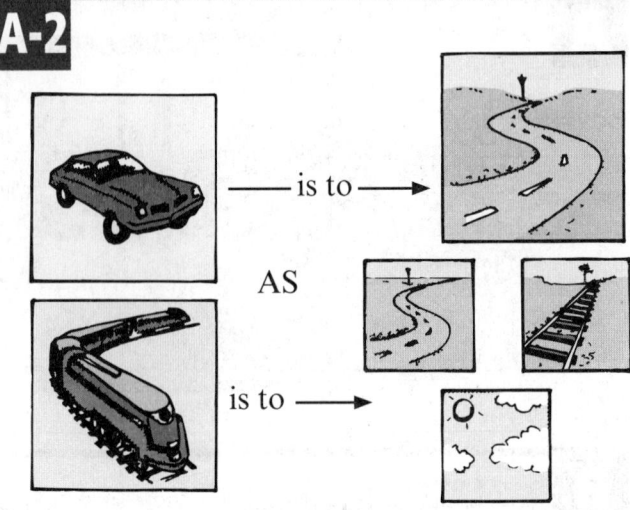

B

1.	true	false	maybe	**4.**	true	false	maybe
2.	true	false	maybe	**5.**	true	false	maybe
3.	true	false	maybe	**6.**	true	false	maybe
				7.	true	false	maybe

C

ⓐ ⓑ ⓒ ⓓ

1. _____

2. _____

3. _____

D

1.	true	false	maybe	**4.**	true	false	maybe
2.	true	false	maybe	**5.**	true	false	maybe
3.	true	false	maybe	**6.**	true	false	maybe
				7.	true	false	maybe

A-1

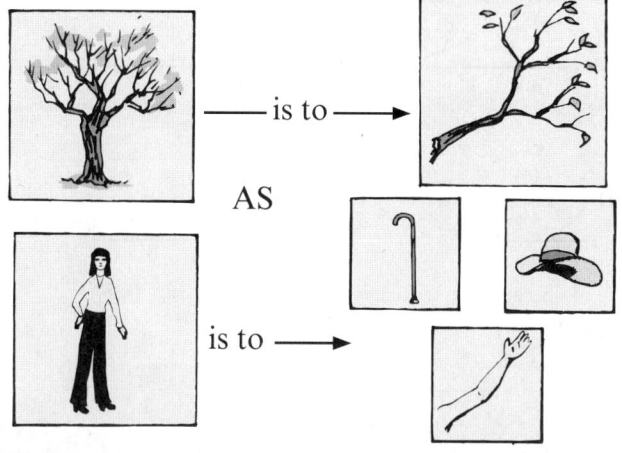

is to

AS

is to

A-2

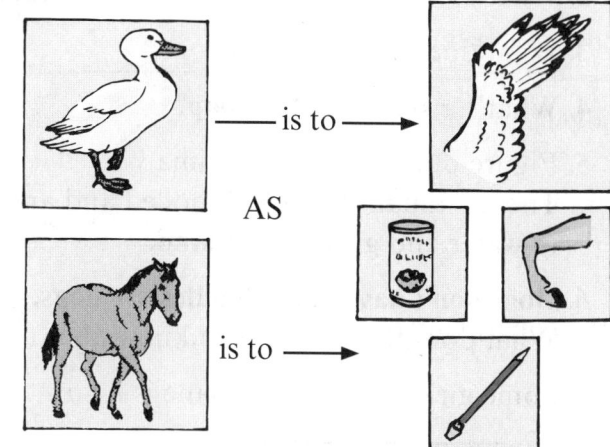

is to

AS

is to

B

ⓐ　　ⓑ　　ⓒ　　ⓓ

1. _____

2. _____

3. _____

C

1. true	false	maybe
2. true	false	maybe
3. true	false	maybe
4. true	false	maybe
5. true	false	maybe
6. true	false	maybe

D

ⓐ　　ⓑ　　ⓒ

E

ⓐ　　ⓑ　　ⓒ

ERRORS

	1	2	3	TOTAL

2. What are all the members of the dog family called?

3. What does **descend** mean?

4. What's a synonym for **jump?**

5. Figure out the class of animals.
   These animals are cold-blooded and are born
   in water and grow up on land.

6. **Dogs don't have gills. Poodles are dogs.**
   What does the rule let you know about poodles?

7. Some girls wear glasses. Jane is a girl.
   So, _____.

8. **Every plant has roots.**
   An emu is an animal.
   What does the rule let you know about an emu?

9. Figure out the class of animals.
   These animals are cold-blooded and have gills.

10. Figure out the class of animals.
    These animals are warm-blooded and have feathers.

11. What's a synonym for a **cat?**

12. What's a synonym for **change?**

A

ⓐ   ⓑ   ⓒ

1. _____
2. _____
3. _____
4. _____

B-1

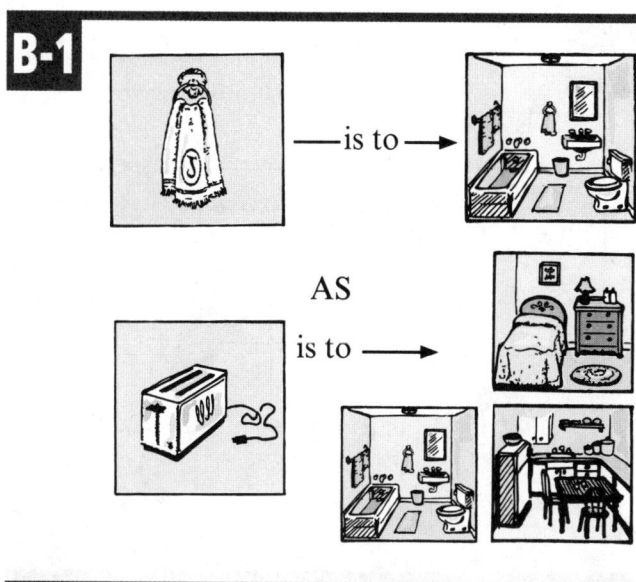

—is to→

AS

is to→

B-2

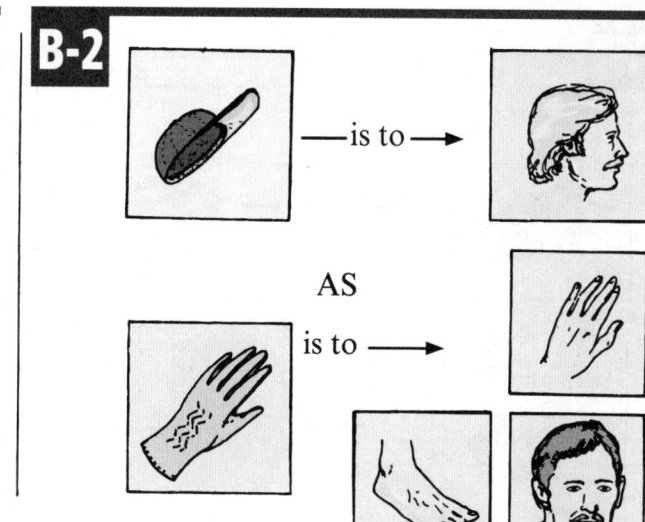

—is to→

AS

is to→

C

ⓐ ⓑ ⓒ

D

ⓐ ⓑ ⓒ ⓓ

1. _____
2. _____
3. _____

E

1. true	false	maybe
2. true	false	maybe
3. true	false	maybe
4. true	false	maybe
5. true	false	maybe
6. true	false	maybe

ERRORS

1	2	3	4	TOTAL

A-1

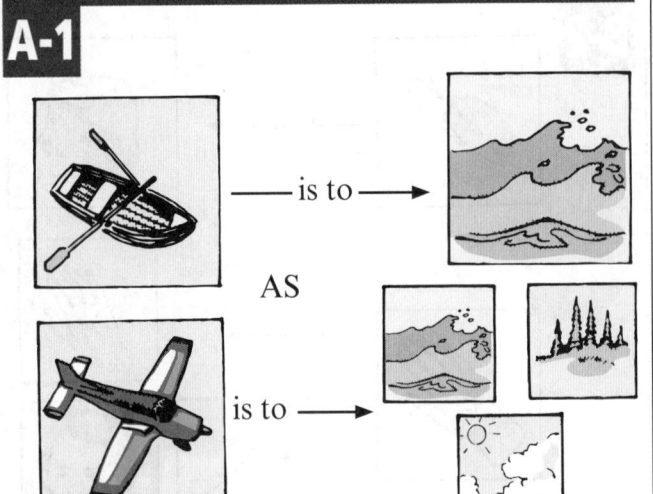

is to

AS

is to

A-2

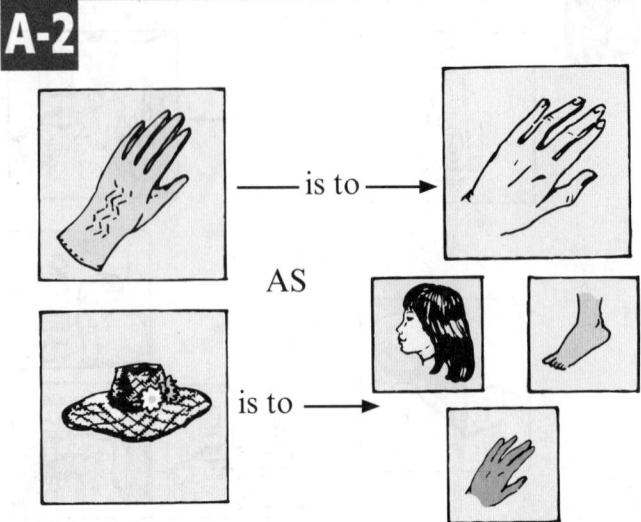

is to

AS

is to

B

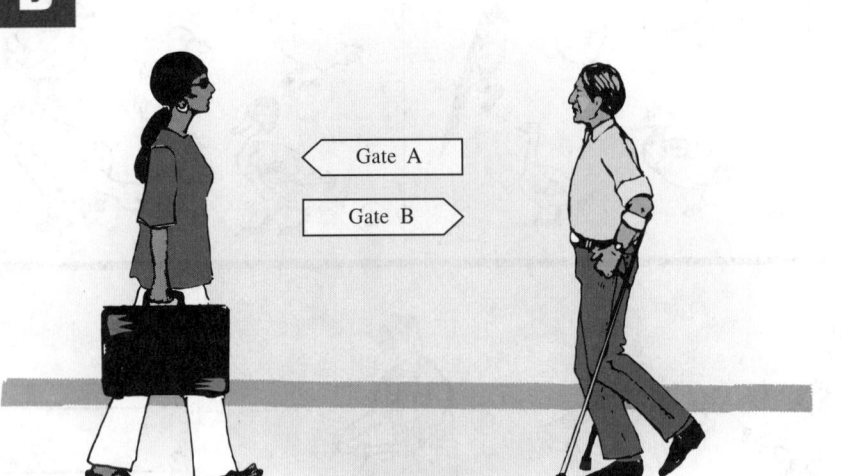

Gate A

Gate B

1. true   false   maybe

2. true   false   maybe

3. true   false   maybe

4. true   false   maybe

5. true   false   maybe

6. true   false   maybe

7. true   false   maybe

C

ⓐ   ⓑ   ⓒ   ⓓ

1. _____

2. _____

3. _____

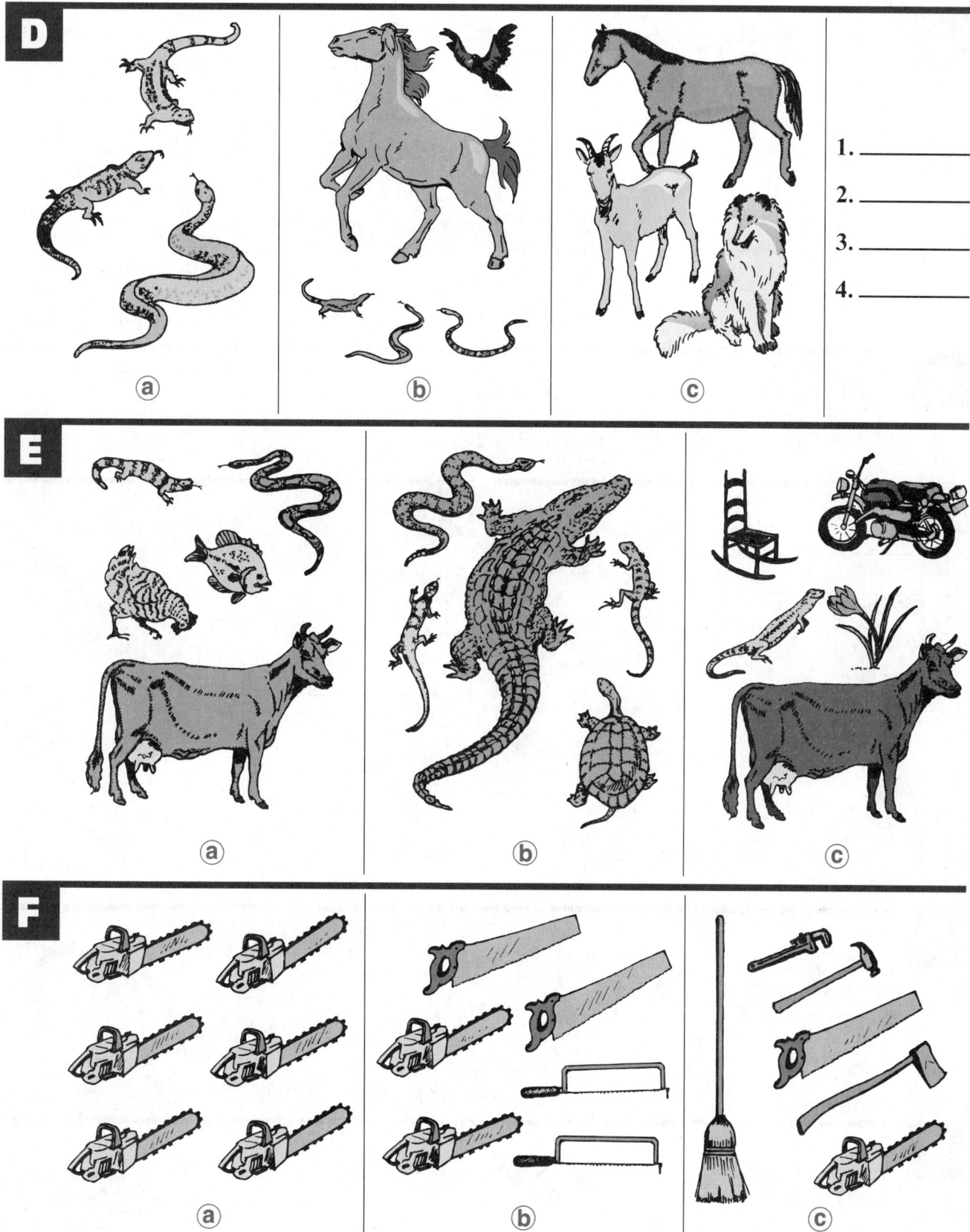

D

ⓐ ⓑ ⓒ

1. _____
2. _____
3. _____
4. _____

E

ⓐ ⓑ ⓒ

F

ⓐ ⓑ ⓒ

ERRORS

1	2	3	4	TOTAL

A

1. true	false	maybe
2. true	false	maybe
3. true	false	maybe
4. true	false	maybe
5. true	false	maybe
6. true	false	maybe

B

C-1

 → is to →

AS

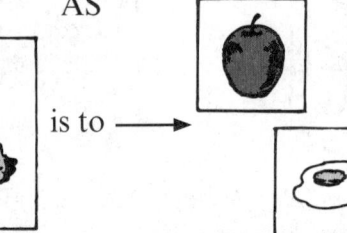 is to →

C-2

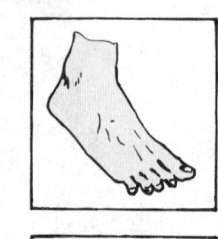 → is to →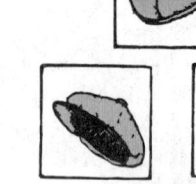

AS

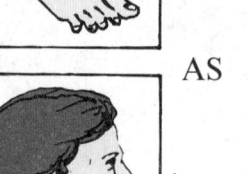 is to →

D

 ⓐ  ⓑ  ⓒ

E

 ⓐ  ⓑ  ⓒ

ERRORS

1	2	3	4	TOTAL

A

1. true false maybe

2. true false maybe

3. true false maybe

4. true false maybe

5. true false maybe

6. true false maybe

7. true false maybe

B

 ⓐ

 ⓑ

 ⓒ

1. _____

2. _____

3. _____

4. _____

C-1

 is to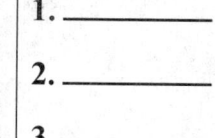

AS

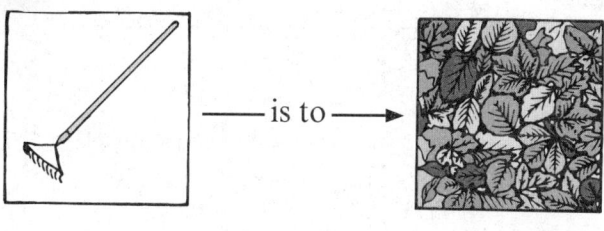 is to

C-2

 is to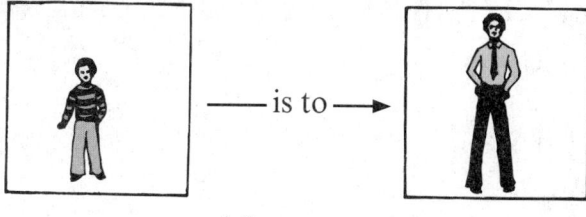

AS

is to

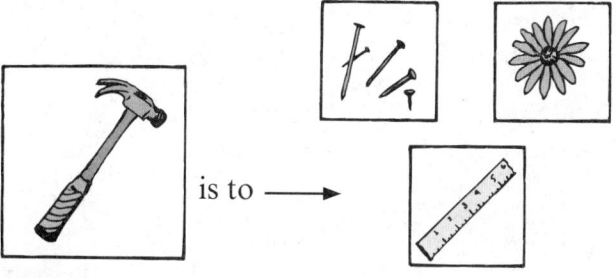

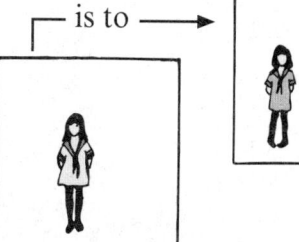

D

ⓐ   ⓑ   ⓒ   ⓓ

1. _____

2. _____

3. _____

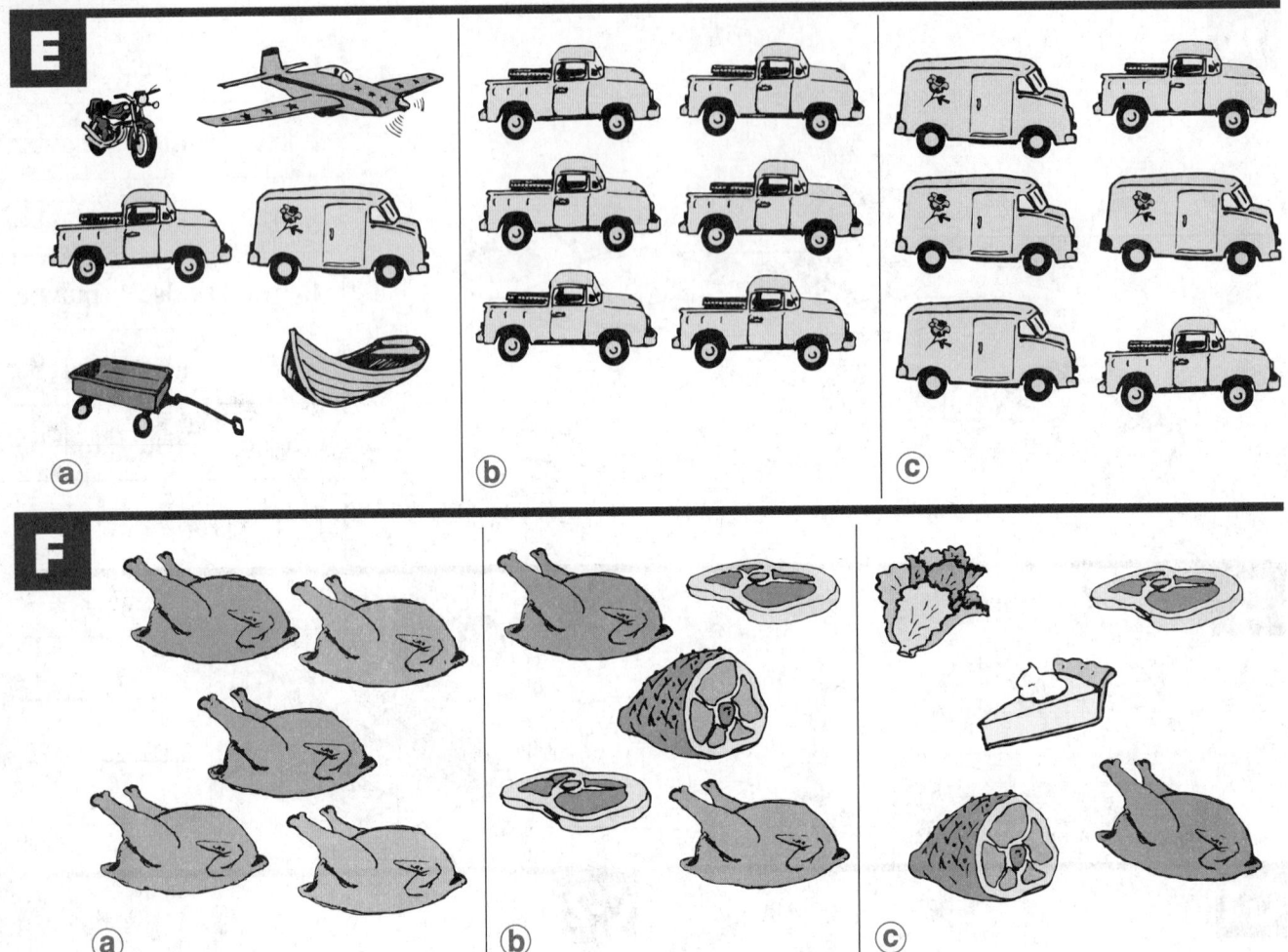

E
(a) (b) (c)

F
(a) (b) (c)

ERRORS

1	2	3	4	TOTAL

A

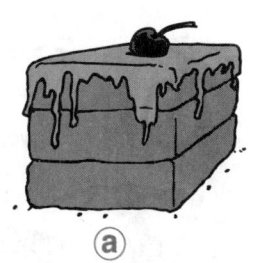 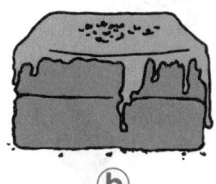  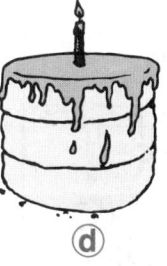

ⓐ   ⓑ   ⓒ   ⓓ

1. _____
2. _____
3. _____

B-1

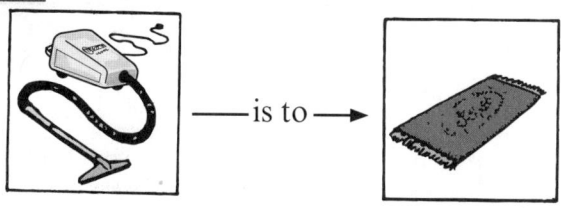

is to →

AS

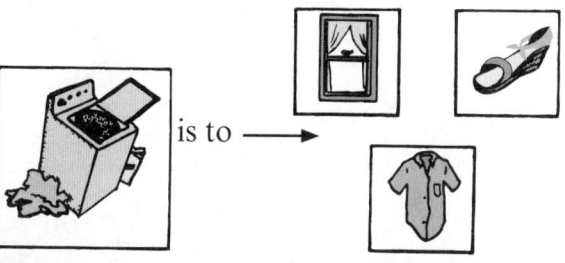

is to →

B-2

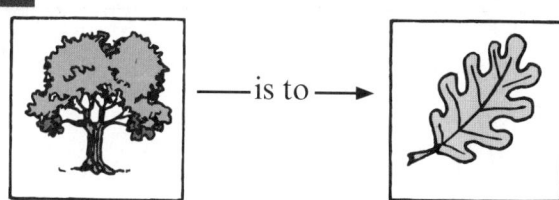

is to →

AS

is to →

C

1.	true	false	maybe
2.	true	false	maybe
3.	true	false	maybe
4.	true	false	maybe
5.	true	false	maybe
6.	true	false	maybe

D

ⓐ   ⓑ   ⓒ

A

ⓐ　　　　　　　　　ⓑ　　　　　　　　　ⓒ

TEST 2

A

1.	true	false	maybe
2.	true	false	maybe
3.	true	false	maybe
4.	true	false	maybe
5.	true	false	maybe
6.	true	false	maybe

B

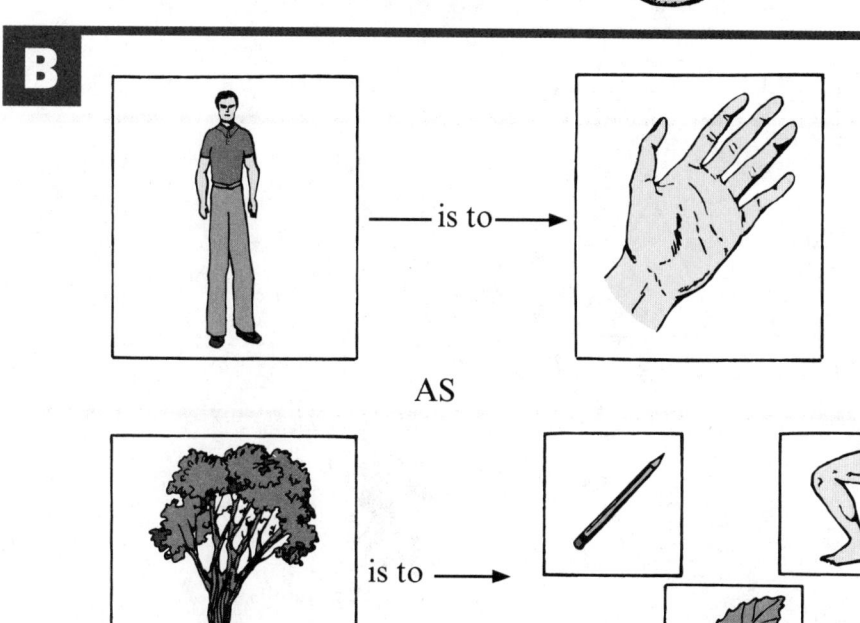

—is to—→

AS

is to—→

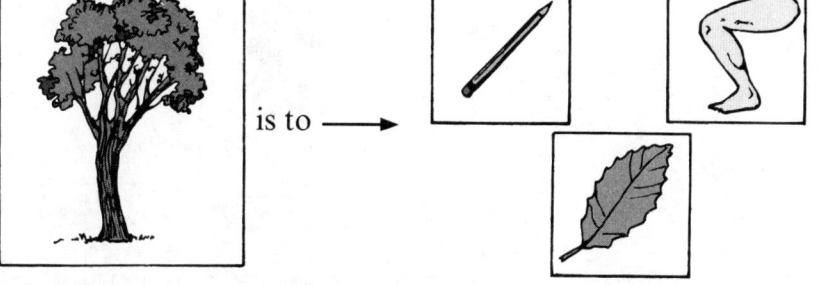

C

 ⓐ    ⓑ    ⓒ    ⓓ

1. _____
2. _____
3. _____

D   **1.** Pass   Fail

E   **1.** Pass   Fail   **2.** Pass   Fail   **3.** Pass   Fail

Test 2   **51**

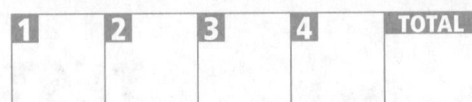

ERRORS

1	2	3	4	TOTAL

A

Write **true**, **false**, or **maybe**.

> Here's the only thing Fred did.
> Fred shined the long shoes.

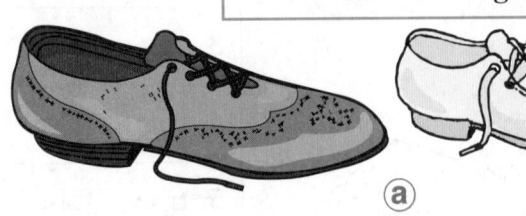

1. Fred shined object B. _____

2. Fred shined object C. _____

3. Fred did not shine object D. _____

B

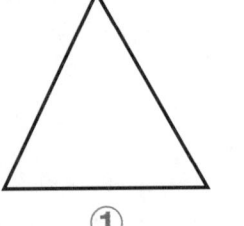 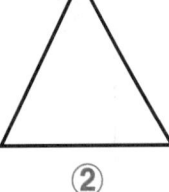 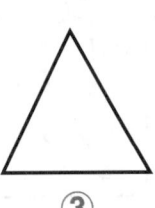

①   ②   ③   ④   ⑤

C

is to

AS

is to

D

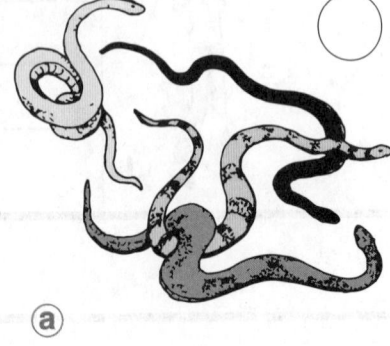 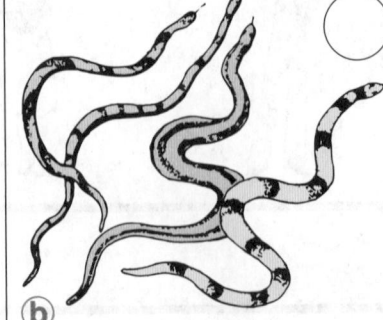 

ⓐ   ⓑ   ⓒ

_____   _____   _____

reptiles   striped snakes   snakes

A Write **true, false,** or **maybe.**

> **Here's the only thing Ann did.**
> **Ann built the short tables.**

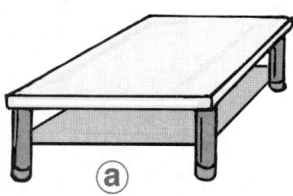 ⓐ ⓑ 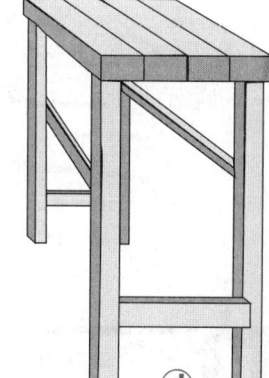 ⓒ ⓓ

1. Ann built object B. _____

2. Ann did not build object C. _____

3. Ann did not build object D. _____

B

☐ ① ☐ ② ☐ ③ ④ ⑤

C

is to   AS   is to

D

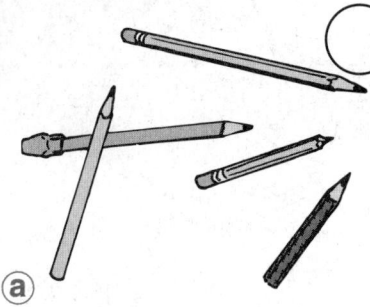 ⓐ

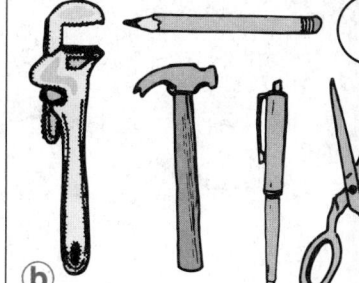 ⓑ

 ⓒ

_____ _____ _____

        tools   writing tools   pencils

ERRORS

1	2	3	4	TOTAL

A

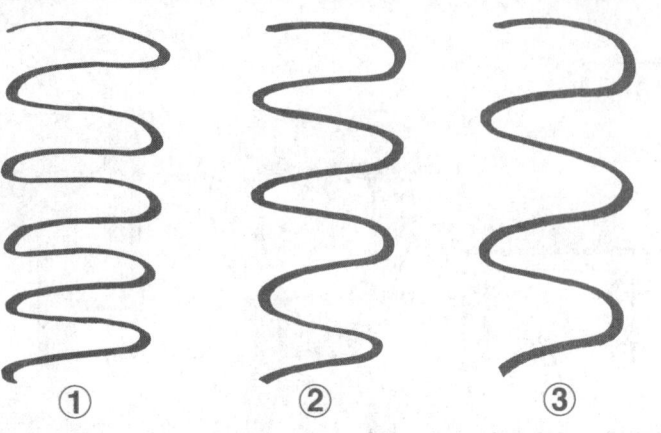

① ② ③ ④ ⑤

B

Write **true, false,** or **maybe.**

> **Here's the only thing the woman did.**
> **The woman wore some of the tall hats.**

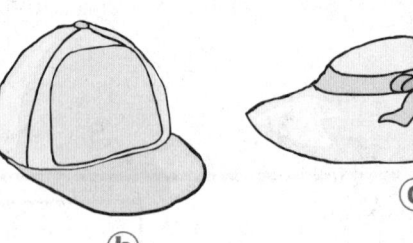

ⓐ ⓑ ⓒ ⓓ

1. The wore object A. _____

2. The woman wore object D. _____

3. The woman did not wear object D. _____

C

Write **true, false,** or **maybe.**

> **Here's the only thing the fire did.**
> **The fire burned fat logs.**

ⓐ ⓑ ⓒ ⓓ

1. The fire burned object A. _____

2. The fire did not burn object B. _____

3. The fire burned object C. _____

D

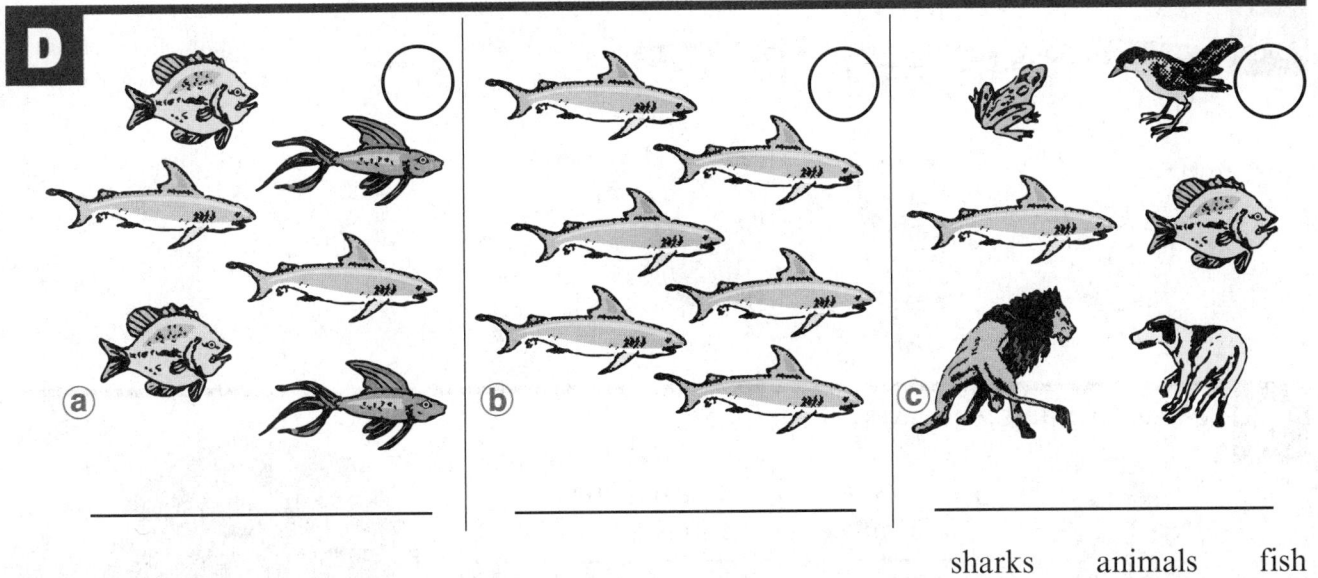

(a)　(b)　(c)

sharks　animals　fish

E

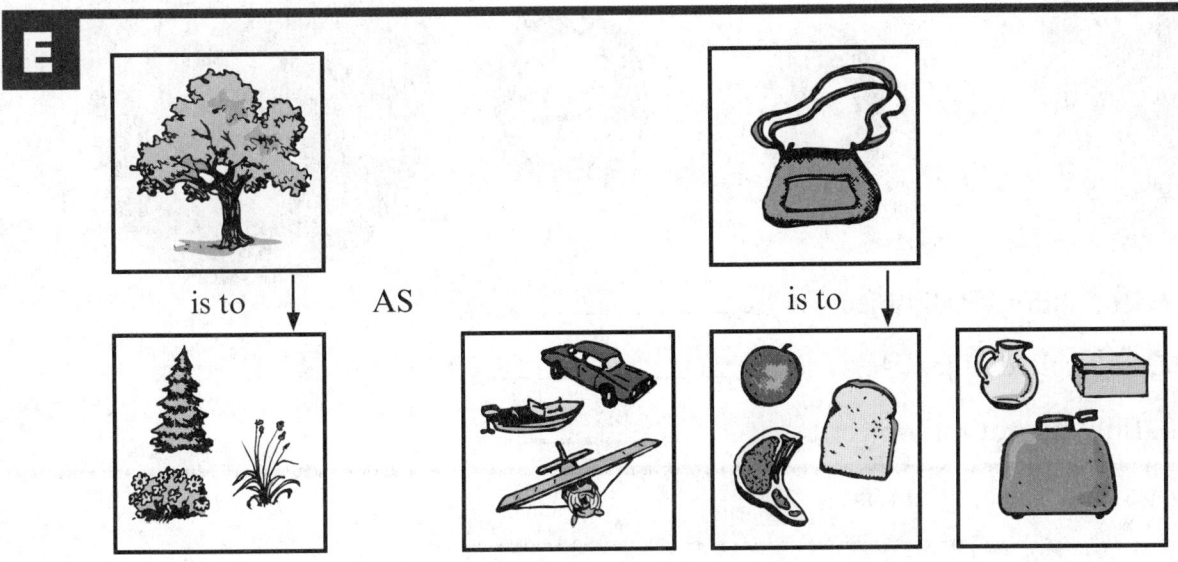

is to　AS　is to

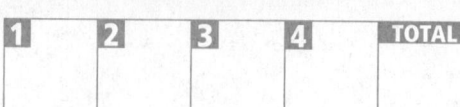

Lesson 34

ERRORS

1	2	3	4	TOTAL

A

① ② ③ ④ ⑤

B

Write **true, false,** or **maybe.**

ⓐ

> **Here's the only thing Bob did.**
> **Bob rolled the tall wheels.**

 ⓑ    ⓒ    ⓓ

1. Bob did not roll object A. _____

2. Bob rolled object A. _____

3. Bob did not roll object D. _____

C

Write **true, false,** or **maybe.**

> **Here's the only thing Mary did.**
> **Mary read some of the wide books.**

ⓐ
ⓑ   ⓒ    ⓓ

1. Mary read object A. _____

2. Mary read object C. _____

3. Mary did not read object D. _____

56 *Lesson 34*

D

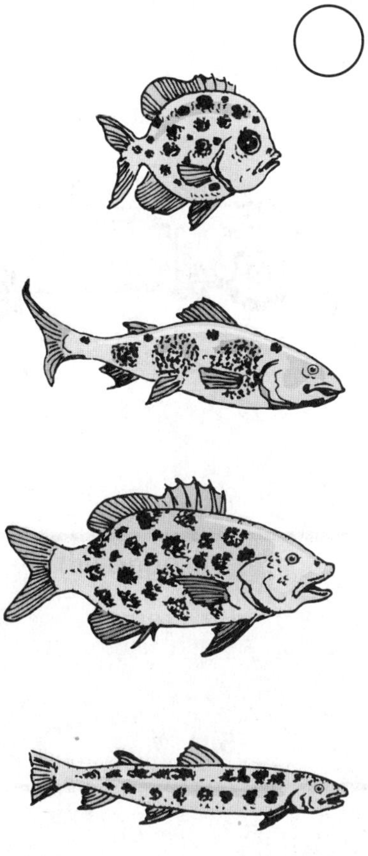

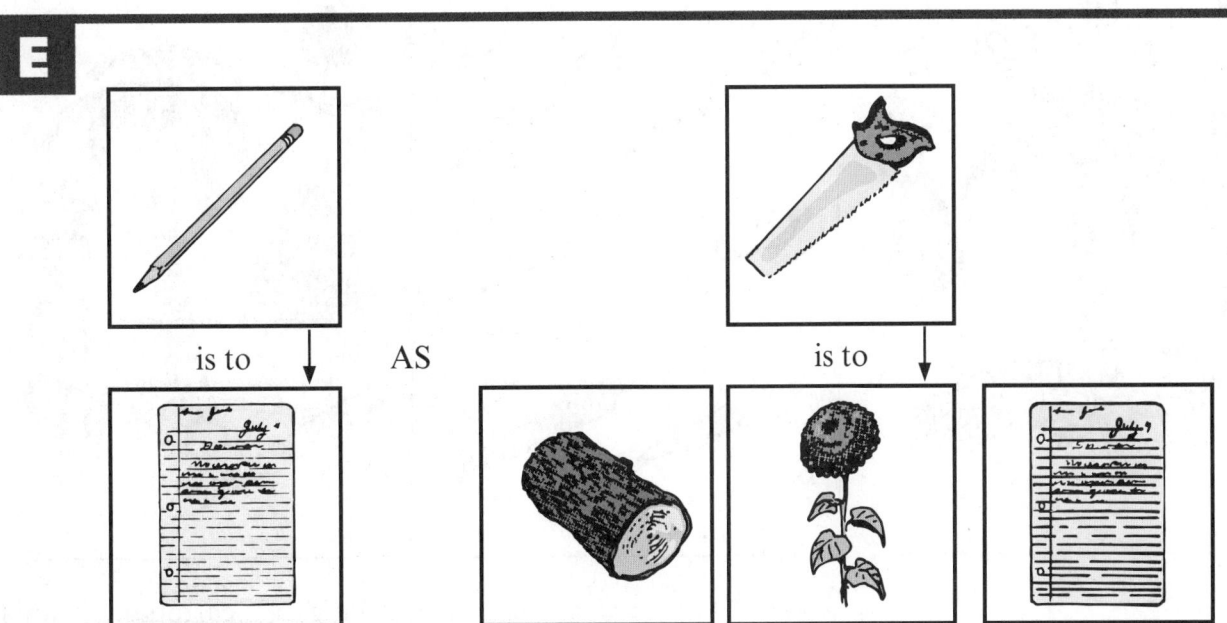

⓪a ⓑb ⓒc

_____   _____   _____

animals   spotted fish   fish

E

is to → AS   is to →

Lesson 35

ERRORS	1	2	3	4	TOTAL

A Write **true**, **false**, or **maybe**.

> **Here's the only thing we know about Fred.**
> **Fred did not drive the long cars.**

ⓐ   ⓑ   ⓒ

1. Fred drove object C. _____

2. Fred drove object B. _____

3. Fred drove object A. _____

B

         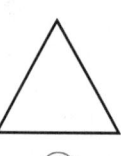

①   ②   ③   ④   ⑤

C Complete the analogy.

A bird is to flying as a fish is to _____.

walking
swimming
talking

D

ⓐ

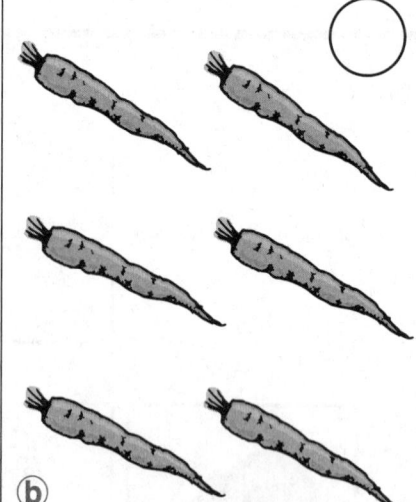

ⓑ

ⓒ

_____   _____   _____

living things   carrots   plants

58   *Lesson 35*

ERRORS

1	**2**	**3**	TOTAL

2. What's a synonym for **big?**

3. Tell the date of New Year's Day.

4. What's a synonym for **healthy?**

5. Listen to the deduction.
Some animals fly.
A dolphin is an animal.
So, _____.
Say the whole deduction.

6. Finish this analogy.
Skinny is to thin as under is to _____.

7. No fish have hair. A salmon is a fish.
What does the rule let you know about a salmon?

8. What's a synonym for **wreck?**

9. Tell the date of Independence Day.

10. Finish this analogy. **A robin is to**
flying as a fish is to _____.

11. What's a synonym for **fast?**

12. What word means **get bigger?**

A	Complete the analogy.

A horse is to mammals as an owl is to _____.

fish
birds
reptiles

B

a _____   b _____   c _____

amphibians   frogs   animals

C   Write **true, false,** or **maybe.**

> **Here's the only thing the dog did.**
> **The dog ate some of the small bones.**

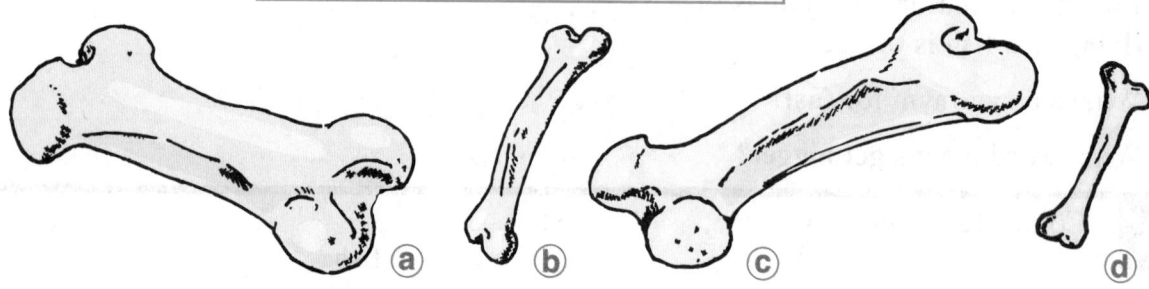

1. The dog ate object A.   _____

2. The dog did not eat object D.   _____

3. The dog ate object B.   _____

D

①   ②   ③   ④   ⑤

A

①	②	③ ④ ⑤

B

Write **true**, **false**, or **maybe**.

Here's the only thing we know about Tom.
Tom did not write with the fat pencils.

ⓐ ⓑ ⓒ ⓓ

1. Tom wrote with object A.   _____

2. Tom wrote with object B.   _____

3. Tom wrote with object C.   _____

C

Complete the analogy.

A man is to a hand as a bear is to a _____.

tail
head
paw

D

ⓐ ⓑ ⓒ

_____   _____   _____

animals   dogs   living things

ERRORS | 1 | 2 | 3 | 4 | TOTAL

A

① ② ③ ④

___ ___ ___ ___
___ ___ ___ ___
___ ___ ___ ___

B

Write **true, false,** or **maybe.**

Here's the only thing we know about Jane.
Jane did not swing the black bats.

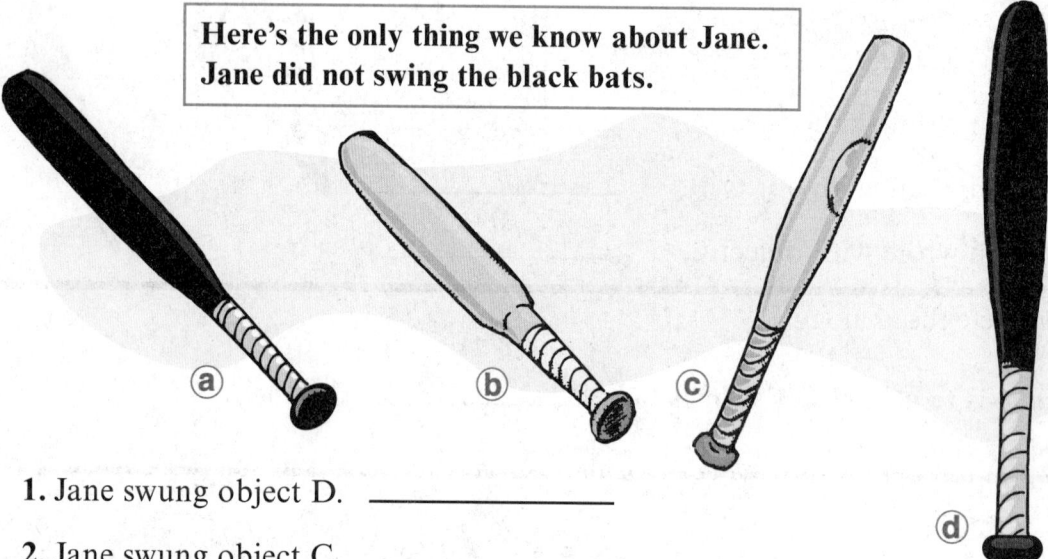

ⓐ ⓑ ⓒ ⓓ

1. Jane swung object D. _____

2. Jane swung object C. _____

3. Jane swung object B. _____

C

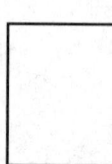

① ② ③ ④ ⑤

D

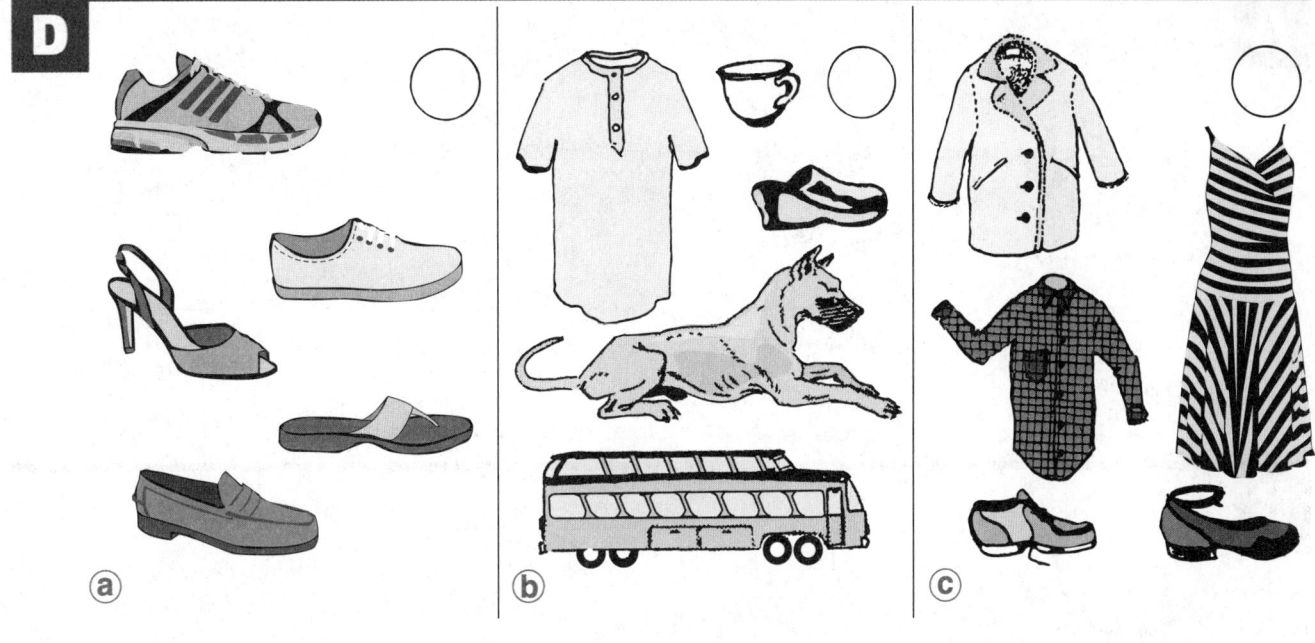

(a) _____

(b) _____

(c) _____

shoes   objects   clothing

E

Complete the analogy.

A pencil is to wood as a nail is to _____.

metal
plastic
paper

ERRORS

1	2	3	4	TOTAL

A

①   ②   ③   ④

___   ___   ___   ___

___   ___   ___   ___

___   ___   ___   ___

B

①   ②   ③   ④   ⑤

C

Grass is to short as a tree is to _____.

fat

tall

short

D

   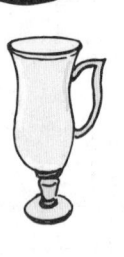 

ⓐ   ⓑ   ⓒ

_____   _____

containers   cups   objects

E

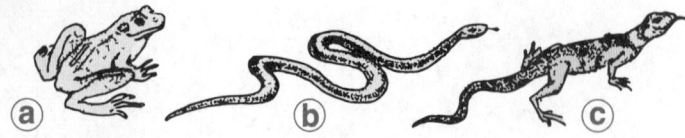 

ⓐ   ⓑ   ⓒ   ⓓ

1. _____

2. _____

3. _____

ERRORS

| 1 | 2 | 3 | 4 | TOTAL |

A

 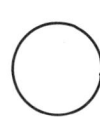 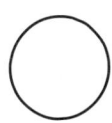

  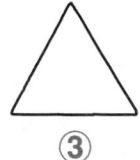

① ② ③ ④ ⑤

B

① ② ③ ④ ⑤

P – men
Z – tall men
D – men wearing hats
L – short men
R – men wearing jackets
B – men without hats
C – men without jackets

_____   _____   _____   _____   _____

_____   _____   _____   _____   _____

_____   _____   _____   _____   _____

_____   _____   _____   _____   _____

C

A hammer is to tools as meat is to _____.

food
red
soft

D

ⓐ   ⓑ   ⓒ   ⓓ

1. _____
2. _____
3. _____

Lesson 40

A

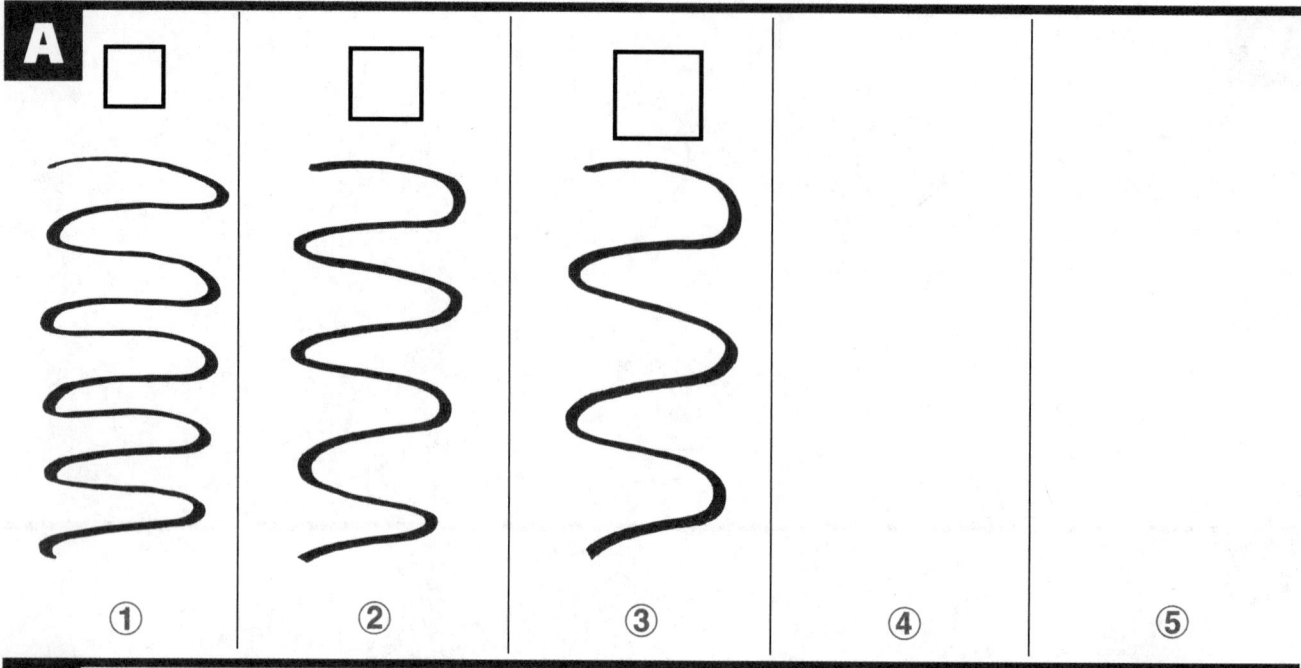

① ② ③ ④ ⑤

B Write **true**, **false**, or **maybe**.

> **Here's the only thing John did.**
> **John planted some tall trees.**

 ⓐ    ⓑ    ⓒ    ⓓ

1. John planted object C. _____

2. John did not plant object A. _____

3. John planted object B. _____

TEST 3

ERRORS

TOTAL

A

① ② ③ ④ ⑤

B

ⓐ ⓑ ⓒ

_____   _____   _____

containers   objects   glasses

C

Write **true, false,** or **maybe.**

> **Here's the only thing Terry did.**
> **Terry made some of the small bowls.**

 ⓐ  ⓑ  ⓒ 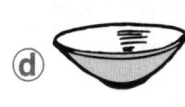 ⓓ

1. Terry made object D.   _____

2. Terry made object B.   _____

3. Terry did not make object C. _____

D

Book is to paper as car is to _____.

paper
plastic
metal

E

1. Pass   Fail

F

1. Pass   Fail   **3.** Pass   Fail
2. Pass   Fail   **4.** Pass   Fail

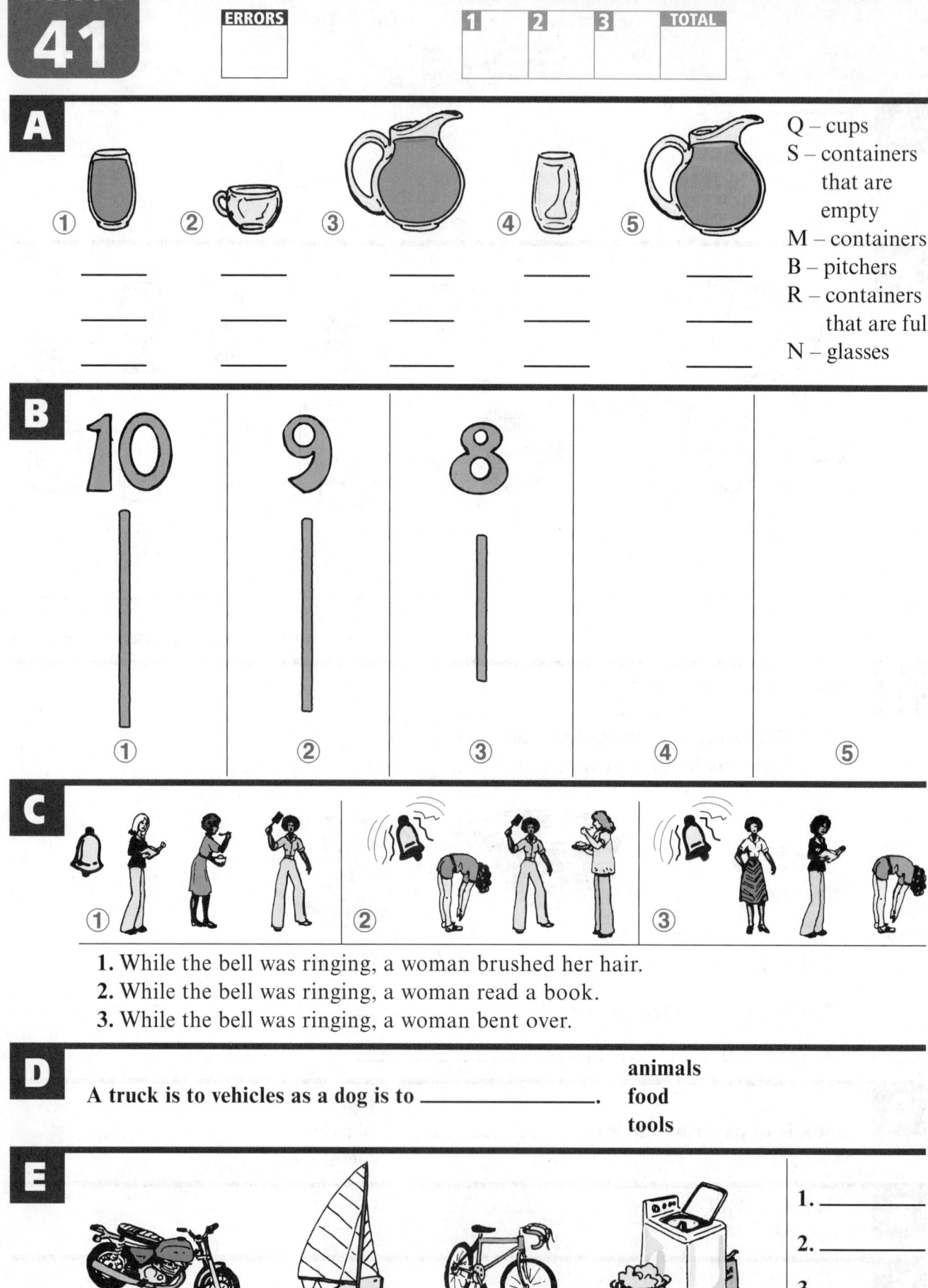

A

① ② ③ ④ ⑤

Q – cups
S – containers
    that are
    empty
M – containers
B – pitchers
R – containers
    that are full
N – glasses

B

10 9 8

① ② ③ ④ ⑤

C

① ② ③

1. While the bell was ringing, a woman brushed her hair.
2. While the bell was ringing, a woman read a book.
3. While the bell was ringing, a woman bent over.

D

A truck is to vehicles as a dog is to _____.

animals
food
tools

E

ⓐ ⓑ ⓒ ⓓ

1. _____
2. _____
3. _____

ERRORS

	1	2	3	4	TOTAL

A

① ② ③ ④ ⑤

E – food
I – foods that are in a pan
O – foods that are on a plate
U – foods that are round
A – fried eggs
B – foods that are long

B

1. While the fire was burning, a man wore a coat.
2. While the fire was burning, a man chopped wood.
3. While the fire was burning, a man wore a hat.

C

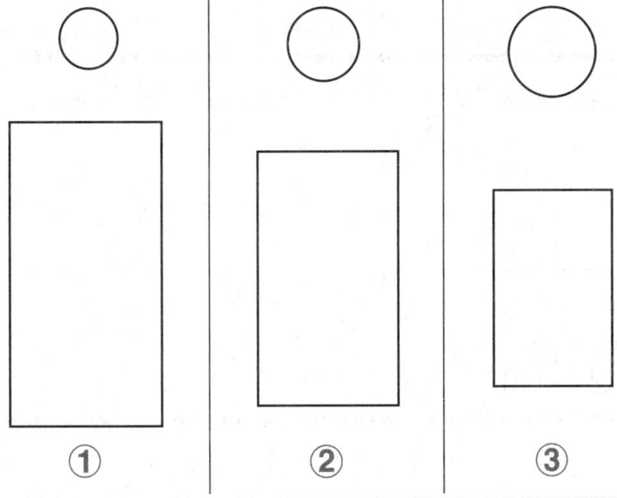

① ② ③ ④ ⑤

D

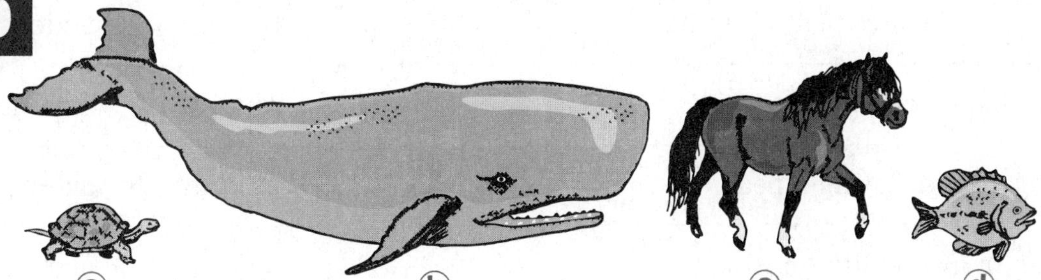

ⓐ ⓑ ⓒ ⓓ

1. _____
2. _____
3. _____

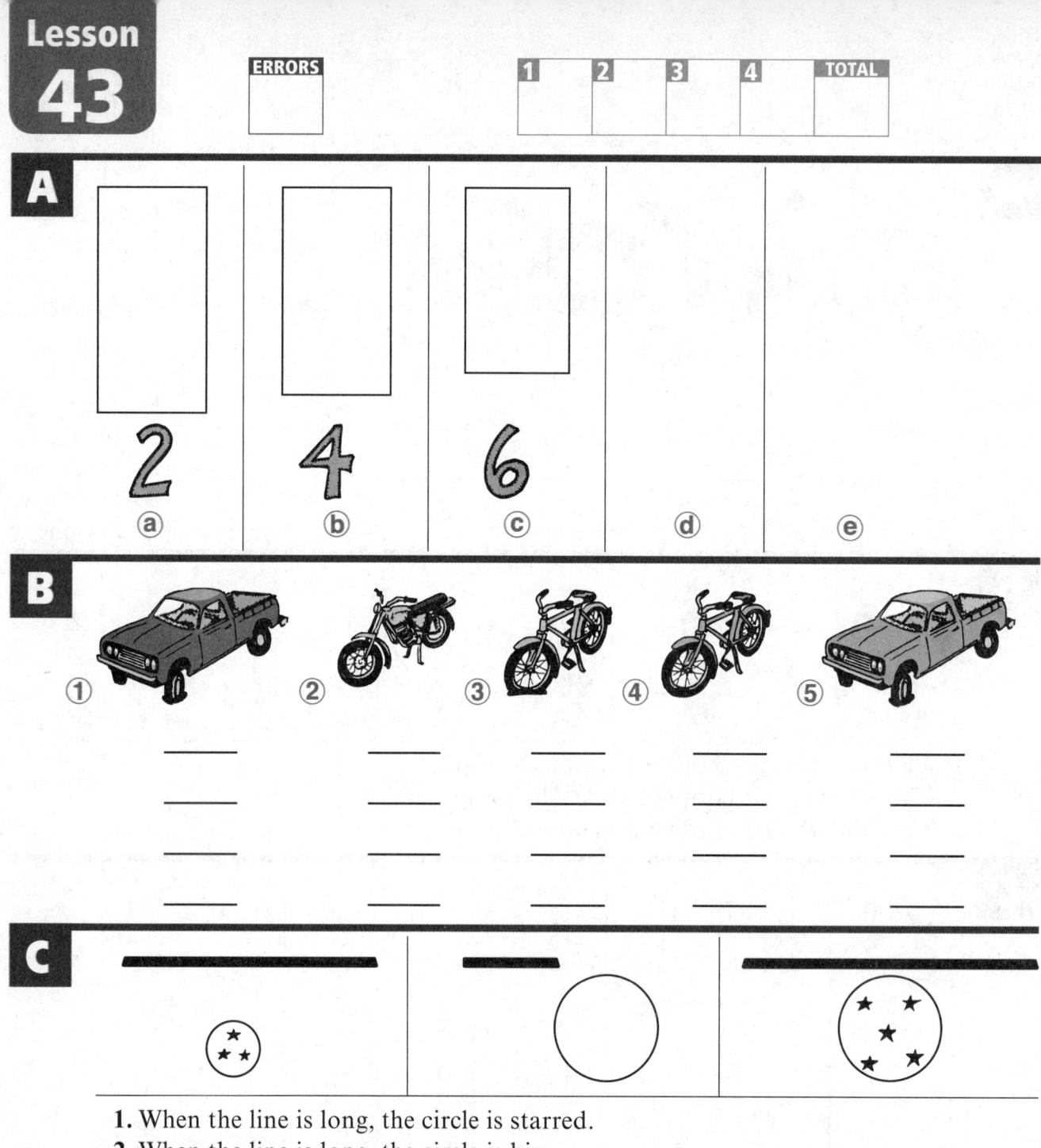

A

2 ⓐ 4 ⓑ 6 ⓒ ⓓ ⓔ

B

① ② ③ ④ ⑤

C

1. When the line is long, the circle is starred.
2. When the line is long, the circle is big.
3. When the line is long, the circle is small.

D

1. ball, elephant, man, sister, cup	objects	actions
2. sleeping, run, stopped, jumping	objects	actions
3. book, paper, car, giraffe, desk	objects	actions
4. sitting, stand, eating a pear	objects	actions
5. hiding in a box, slid, masticate	objects	actions

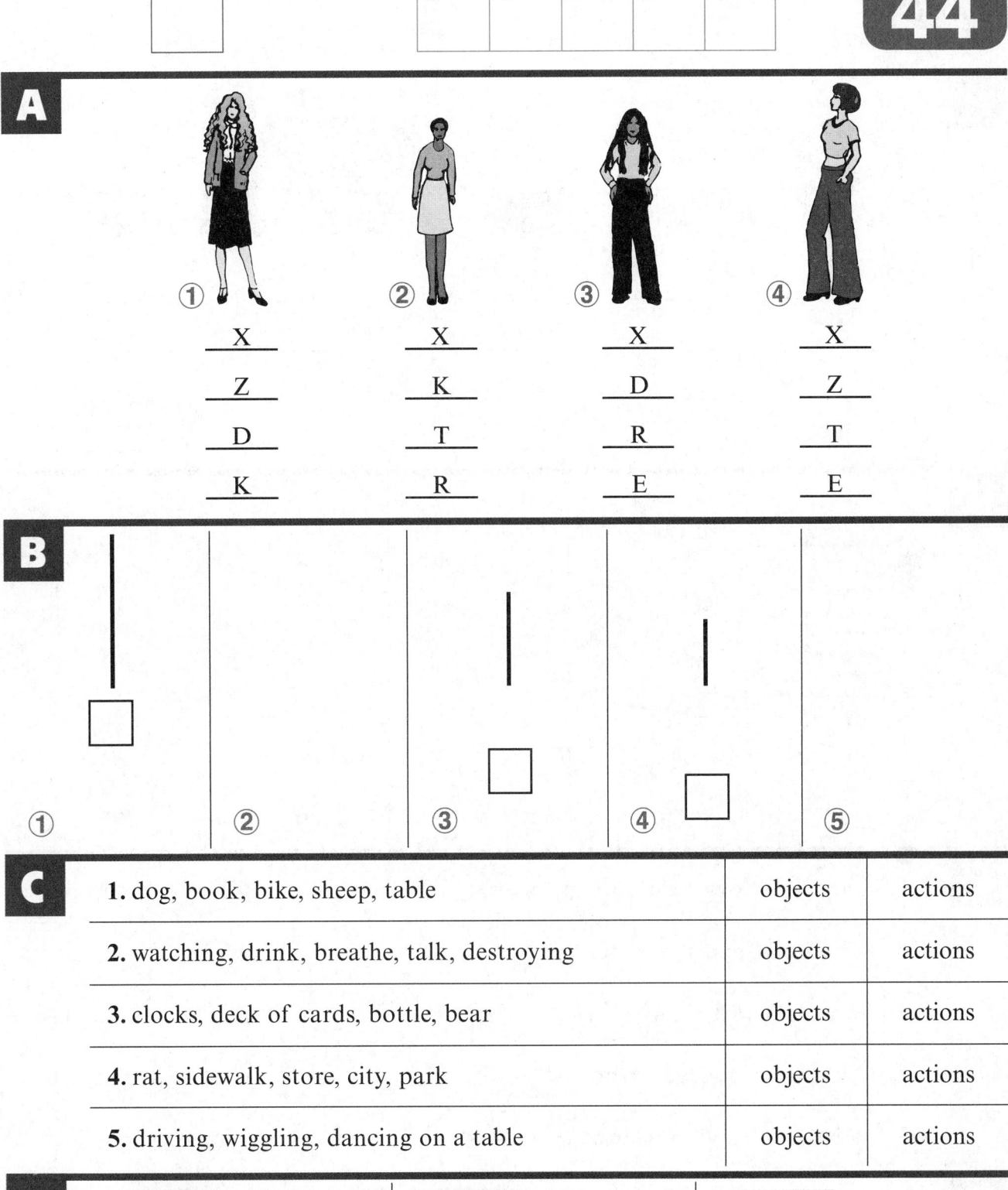

A

① X Z D K

② X K T R

③ X D R E

④ X Z T E

B

① ② ③ ④ ⑤

C

1. dog, book, bike, sheep, table	objects	actions
2. watching, drink, breathe, talk, destroying	objects	actions
3. clocks, deck of cards, bottle, bear	objects	actions
4. rat, sidewalk, store, city, park	objects	actions
5. driving, wiggling, dancing on a table	objects	actions

D

1. When the square is striped, the triangle is little.
2. When the square is striped, the triangle is large.
3. When the square is striped, the triangle is dotted.

ERRORS | 1 | 2 | 3 | 4 | **TOTAL**

A

 ①  ②  ③  ④  ⑤

___ ___ ___ ___

___ ___ ___ ___

___ ___ ___ ___

___ ___ ___ ___

B

 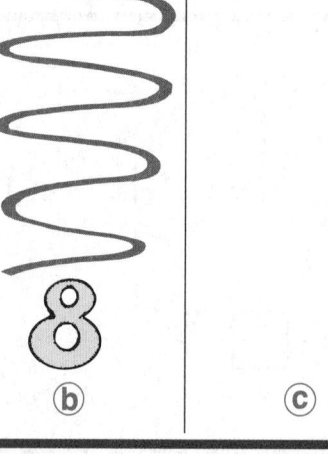 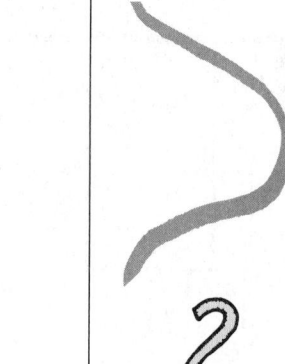

ⓐ ⓑ ⓒ ⓓ ⓔ

C

1. standing on your head, slipping, snoring	objects	actions
2. shoes, truck, pants, box, pen	objects	actions
3. lighting a match, ignore, chew	objects	actions
4. yelling, singing a song, read	objects	actions
5. football, towel, glass, magazine	objects	actions

D

1. Each time the cow was in the barn, it ate hay.
2. Each time the cow was in the barn, it mooed.
3. Each time the cow was outside, it ate hay.

ERRORS

1	2	3	TOTAL

2. What's the opposite of **outside?**

3. What word means **look at?**

4. What's the opposite of **young?**

5. Name the holiday that comes at the end of November.

6. What word means **eat** or **use up?**

7. Finish this analogy.
Full is to empty as quiet is to _____.

8. Chair. **Object** or **action?**

9. What's a synonym for **understand?**

10. What's the opposite of **rough?**

11. Sitting in a chair. **Object** or **action?**

12. What's a synonym for **show?**

A

① ② ③ ④ ⑤

B

① ② ③ ④

_____ _____ _____ _____

_____ _____ _____ _____

C

1. cat, stove, jug of milk, pliers		objects	actions
2. obtain, riding a bike, sit, eating		objects	actions
3. pencils, cup, window, pair of shoes		objects	actions
4. drinking milk, modify, buying, instruct		objects	actions
5. swinging, write, sweep, cooking dinner		objects	actions

D

1. When it rained, the cat chased a bird.
2. When it rained, the cat climbed a tree.
3. When the sun was out, the cat climbed a tree.

ERRORS

1	2	3	4	TOTAL

A

① ② ③ ④ ⑤

①	②	③	④	⑤
B	B	B	B	B
C	D	C	C	D
F	F	A	F	A
G	E	H	G	E
E		E		

B

① ② ③ ④ ⑤

C

1. desk, squirrel, balloon, bag, lion	objects	actions
2. sleep, watching, throw, drop	objects	actions
3. chew, study, see, typing	objects	actions
4. scratching, amble, traveling on a bus	objects	actions
5. hamburger, jacket, newspaper, rug, bug	objects	actions

D

1. When the rectangle is long, the circle is dotted.
2. When the rectangle is dotted, the circle is big.
3. When the rectangle is short, the square is dotted.

ERRORS

1	2	3	4	TOTAL

A

1. When the moon was half full, a tiger roared.
2. When the moon was half full, a tiger chased a butterfly.
3. When the moon was half full, a tiger drank from a river.

B

ⓐ   ⓑ   ⓒ

_____   _____   _____

human beings   women   mammals

C

A pen is to writing as a knife is to _____.
     blade
     handle
     cutting

D

1. reading, wearing a coat, descend, go	objects	actions
2. drinking coffee, pull, fall, seeing	objects	actions
3. coffee, bus, coats, airplane, sharks	objects	actions
4. talking, duplicate, sipping a milkshake	objects	actions
5. popcorn, milkshake, notebook, canine	objects	actions

E

ERRORS

1	2	3	4	TOTAL

A   ① ② ③ ④ ⑤

___ ___ ___ ___ ___

___ ___ ___ ___ ___

___ ___ ___ ___ ___

                                   ___

B

△   △   △

1. When the line is wavy, the glass is full.
2. When the line is straight, the glass is empty.
3. When the line is straight, the glass is full.

C

1. telephone, dress, car, butterfly, bus	objects	actions
2. talking on a telephone, eating, riding	objects	actions
3. skated, sit, breathe	objects	actions
4. stand up, clean, paddle	objects	actions
5. machine, wagon, cat, pencil, chair	objects	actions

D

ERRORS

	1	2	3	4	TOTAL

A

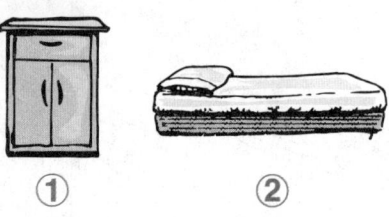

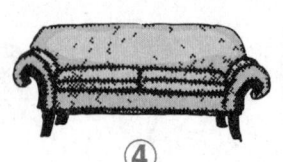
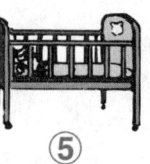

①	②	③	④	⑤	⑥
Z	Z	Z	Z	Z	Z
X	V	Y	Y	Y	Y
T	T	W	W	V	X

B

1. candy, factory, garage, potatoes, bike	objects	actions
2. eat potatoes, sit down, comprehend	objects	actions
3. typing, traveling in a car, swallow	objects	actions
4. move, look, chew, modify	objects	actions
5. hot dog, hat, floor, ship, pen	objects	actions

C

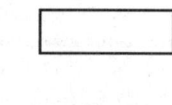
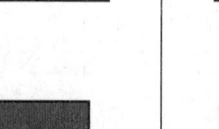
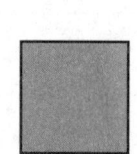

D

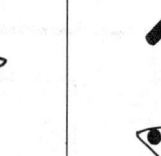
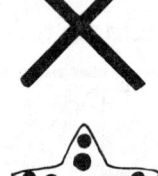

1. When the X is big, the big star is dotted.
2. When the X is small, the star is dotted.
3. When the X is big, the stars are big.

A

1. stretch, listen, consume	objects	actions	tell what kind
2. milk, player, giraffe	objects	actions	tell what kind
3. blue, sleepy, skinny	objects	actions	tell what kind
4. blow, slurp, hear	objects	actions	tell what kind
5. sewing, pull, drive	objects	actions	tell what kind

B

Underline the carnivorous animals.
Circle the herbivorous animals.

ERRORS

TOTAL

TEST 4

A			
1. chair, elephant, pencil, motorcycle	objects	actions
2. frog, television, pillow, woman	objects	actions
3. hop, leap, masticate, cry	objects	actions
4. amble, smile, yell, kick	objects	actions
5. bowl, book, letter, ladder	objects	actions

B

① ② ③ ④ ⑤

C

1. When the line is long, the square is big.
2. When the line is straight, the square is big.
3. When the line is straight, the square is small.

D

1. Pass   Fail

E

1. Pass   Fail

2. Pass   Fail

3. Pass   Fail

F

1. Pass   Fail

1	2	3	4	TOTAL

A

1. When it was spring, the bear slept.
2. When it was spring, the bear ate a fish.
3. When it was winter, the bear slept.

B

1. wear, pick, cough	objects	actions	tell what kind
2. wet, loud, indolent	objects	actions	tell what kind
3. boil, roar, inquire	objects	actions	tell what kind
4. insect, paper clip, jacket	objects	actions	tell what kind
5. mouse, grass, jar	objects	actions	tell what kind

C

Wet is to dry as full is to _____.

quiet
long
empty

D

Write **true, false,** or **maybe.**

> **Here's the only thing we know about Max.**
> **Max chewed none of the small bones.**

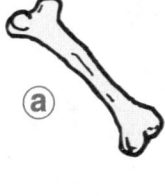 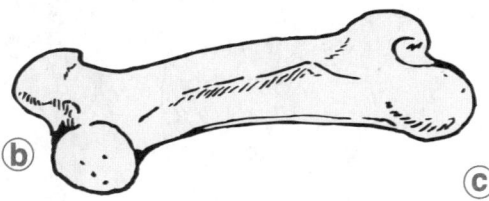 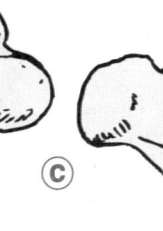 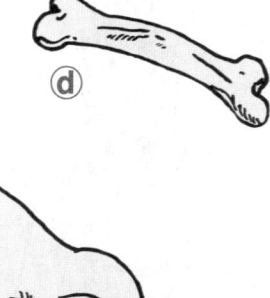

ⓐ ⓑ ⓒ ⓓ

1. Max chewed object A. _____

2. Max chewed object C. _____

3. Max chewed object D. _____

ERRORS

1	2	3	4	TOTAL

A Write **true, false,** or **maybe.**

> Here's the only thing Sue did.
> Sue wore some of the white shirts.

 (a)  (b)  (c)  (d) (e)

1. Sue wore object A. _____

2. Sue did not wear object C. _____

3. Sue wore object D. _____

B

1. motorcycle, ink, lamp	objects	actions	tell what kind
2. hot, sticky, lumpy	objects	actions	tell what kind
3. skates, water, picture	objects	actions	tell what kind
4. mean, happy, quick	objects	actions	tell what kind
5. envelope, flower, shell	objects	actions	tell what kind

C

Christmas is to December as Independence Day is to _____.

June
January
July

D

(a) (b) (c) (d)

1. _____

2. _____

3. _____

A

① ② ③ ④ ⑤

___ ___ ___ ___ ___

___ ___ ___ ___ ___

___ ___ ___ ___ ___

B

	objects	actions	tell what kind
1. furry, tall, round	objects	actions	tell what kind
2. clock, rock, ashes	objects	actions	tell what kind
3. terrible, glad, sloppy	objects	actions	tell what kind
4. read, carry, complete	objects	actions	tell what kind
5. deduce, touch, shut	objects	actions	tell what kind

C Write **true, false,** or **maybe.**

> Here's the only thing we know about Jack.
> Jack did not sit on the short chairs.

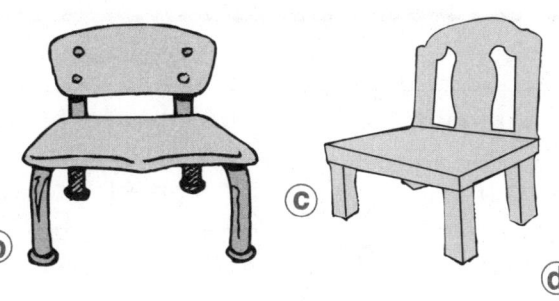

ⓐ ⓑ ⓒ ⓓ

1. Jack sat on object B. _____

2. Jack did not sit on object C. _____

3. Jack sat on object D. _____

D

Winter is to cold as summer is to _____.

dry
hot
cold

ERRORS | 1 | 2 | 3 | 4 | TOTAL

A

① ② ③ ④ ⑤

D	D	D	D	D
F	H	F	H	H
J	J	L	L	J
M	M	O	O	O

B

People are to skin as trees are to _____.   bark   skin   green

C

Write **true, false,** or **maybe.**

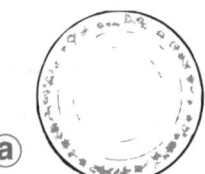

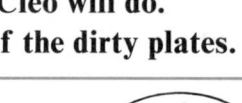

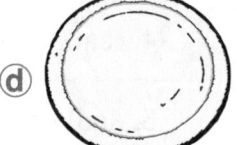

> Here's the only thing Cleo will do.
> Cleo will wash some of the dirty plates.

ⓐ ⓑ ⓒ ⓓ

1. Cleo will wash object B.   _____

2. Cleo will wash object D.   _____

3. Cleo will wash object A.   _____

D

1. dirty, broken, clean	objects	actions	tell what kind
2. clouds, man, mountain	objects	actions	tell what kind
3. flying, sweep, pour	objects	actions	tell what kind
4. hit, fishing, weep	objects	actions	tell what kind
5. leaves, pins, card	objects	actions	tell what kind

E

Make a box around the herbivorous animals.
Circle the carnivorous animals.

A

ⓐ _____

ⓑ _____

ⓒ _____

house cats   felines   mammals

B

1. bounce, catch, run	objects	actions	tell what kind
2. cut, watering, spin	objects	actions	tell what kind
3. pretty, yellow, quiet	objects	actions	tell what kind
4. destroy, complete, masticate	objects	actions	tell what kind
5. indolent, weak, green	objects	actions	tell what kind

C

 ⓐ
 ⓑ
 ⓒ ⓓ

1. _____
2. _____
3. _____

D

Write **true, false,** or **maybe.**

> Here's the only thing Bob did.
> Bob tore the spotted pants.

 ⓐ
 ⓑ
 ⓒ
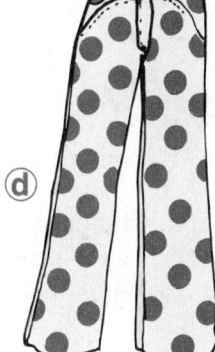 ⓓ

1. Bob tore object C. _____

2. Bob tore object A. _____

3. Bob did not tear object D. _____

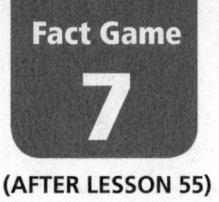

Fact Game

7

(AFTER LESSON 55)

ERRORS | 1 | 2 | 3 | TOTAL

FACT GAME SCORECARD

1	2	3	4	5	6	7	8	9	10	11	12	13	14	15
16	17	18	19	20	21	22	23	24	25	26	27	28	29	30

2. What word means **more than half?**

3. What's the opposite of **dangerous?**

4. What word means **figure out?**

5. What's the opposite of **push?**

6. What's a synonym for **ask?**

7. Some animals eat only plants.
   What are those animals called?

8. What's the opposite of **difficult?**

9. Some animals eat meat.
   What are those animals called?

10. What's the opposite of **soft?**

11. What word means **make** or **build?**

12. What's the opposite of **straight?**

A   Write **true, false,** or **maybe.**

> **Here's the only thing we know about the cat.**
> **The cat climbed none of the short trees.**

ⓐ   ⓑ   ⓒ   ⓓ

1. The cat climbed object D.   _____

2. The cat climbed object C.   _____

3. The cat did not climb object B.   _____

86   *Fact Game 7*

B

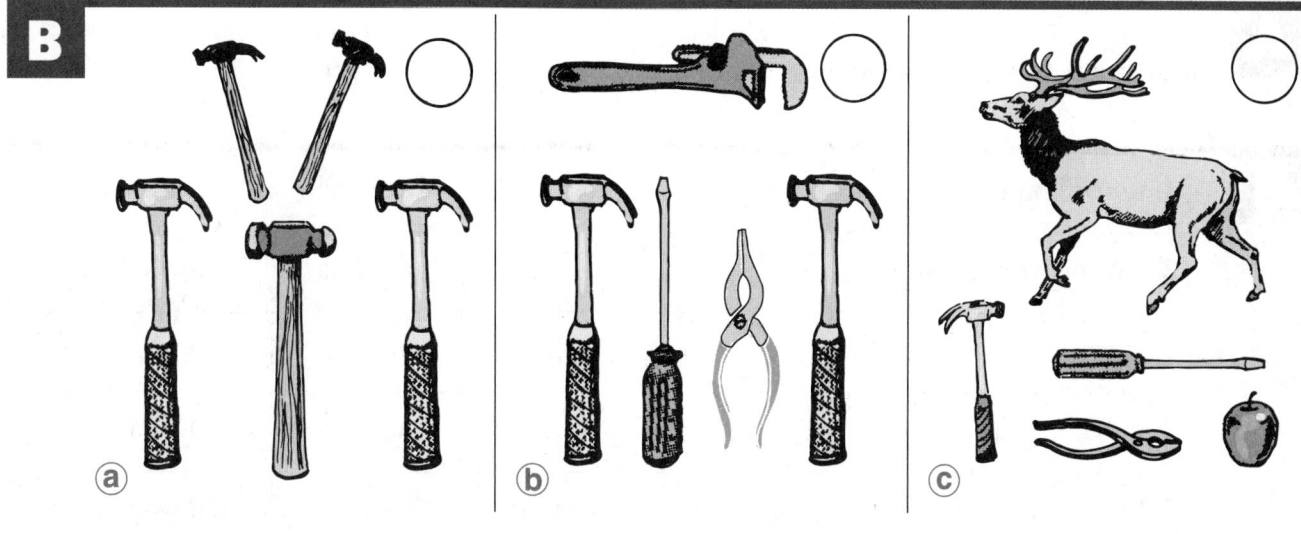

| a | b | c |

_____   _____   _____

tools   objects   hammers

C

a   b   c   d

1. _____
2. _____
3. _____

D

1. green, narrow, shiny	objects	actions	tell what kind
2. lose, start, descend	objects	actions	tell what kind
3. healthy, crooked, easy	objects	actions	tell what kind
4. basket, sun, door	objects	actions	tell what kind
5. destroy, weep, teach	objects	actions	tell what kind

ERRORS | 1 | 2 | 3 | 4 | TOTAL

A

A snake is to reptiles as an eagle is to _____.

mammals
reptiles
birds

B

1. ignore, amble, descend	objects	actions	tell what kind
2. canine, purse, plant	objects	actions	tell what kind
3. runny, difficult, silly	objects	actions	tell what kind
4. modify, leap, instruct	objects	actions	tell what kind
5. feline, containers, tree	objects	actions	tell what kind

C

Write **true, false,** or **maybe.**

Here's the only thing the goat will do.
The goat will eat some cans.

     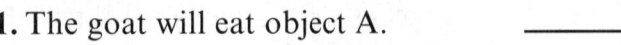 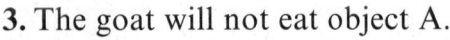 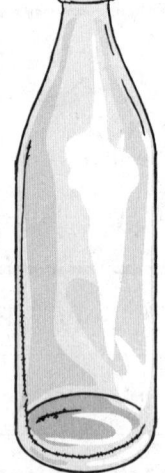

ⓐ   ⓑ   ⓒ   ⓓ

1. The goat will eat object A. _____

2. The goat will eat object D. _____

3. The goat will not eat object A. _____

D

ⓐ   ⓑ   ⓒ   ⓓ

1.

2. _____

3. _____

ERRORS | 1 | 2 | 3 | 4 | TOTAL

A

Write **true, false,** or **maybe.**

> **Here's the only thing we know about Judy.
> Judy rode none of the black horses.**

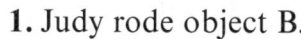

1. Judy rode object B. _____

2. Judy did not ride object A. _____

3. Judy rode object D. _____

B

1. obtain, duplicate, examine	objects	actions	tell what kind
2. large, funny, wild	objects	actions	tell what kind
3. comprehend, exhibit, inquire	objects	actions	tell what kind
4. shiny, dull, striped	objects	actions	tell what kind
5. construct, consume, complete	objects	actions	tell what kind

C

Make a **C** on the carnivorous animals.
Make an **H** on the herbivorous animals.

D

A trout is to fish as a bat is to _____.

birds
mammals
reptiles

E

1. _____

2. _____

3. _____

ERRORS

1	2	3	4	TOTAL

A

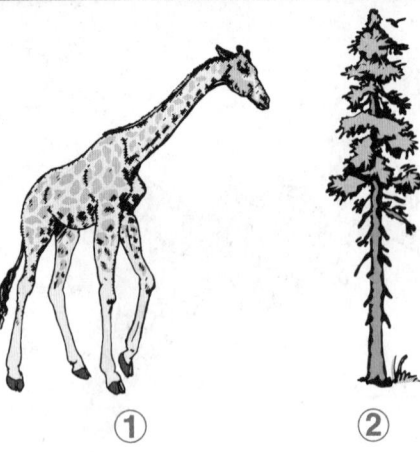

①   ②   ③   ④

___ ___ ___ ___

___ ___ ___ ___

___ ___ ___ ___

B

A leopard is to spots as a zebra is to _____.

stripes
dots
checks

C

1. vehicles, appliance, animal	objects	actions	tell what kind
2. pitcher, stove, bread	objects	actions	tell what kind
3. climb, shout, spell	objects	actions	tell what kind
4. thin, purple, plastic	objects	actions	tell what kind
5. real, hard, soft	objects	actions	tell what kind

D   Write **true, false,** or **maybe.**

> **Here's the only thing Dan did.
> Dan chased some white ducks.**

ⓐ   ⓑ   ⓒ   ⓓ

1. Dan chased object C.   _____

2. Dan did not chase object B.   _____

3. Dan chased object A.   _____

A

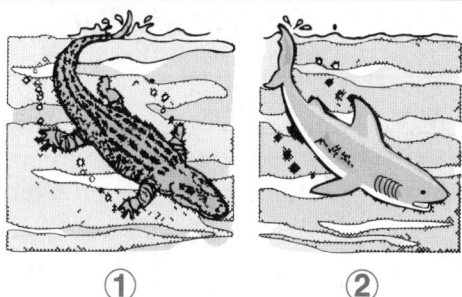

①	②	③	④	⑤
C	C	C	C	C
E	E	G	E	G
J	I	J	I	J
L		L		

B

1. lizard, bat, trunk	objects	actions	tell what kind
2. bathe, tell, modify	objects	actions	tell what kind
3. healthy, sick, dry	objects	actions	tell what kind
4. exhibit, bush, tiger	objects	actions	tell what kind
5. deduce, decrease, dig	objects	actions	tell what kind

C

Write **true, false,** or **maybe.**

> **Here's the only thing Meg did.**
> **Meg dug some deep holes.**

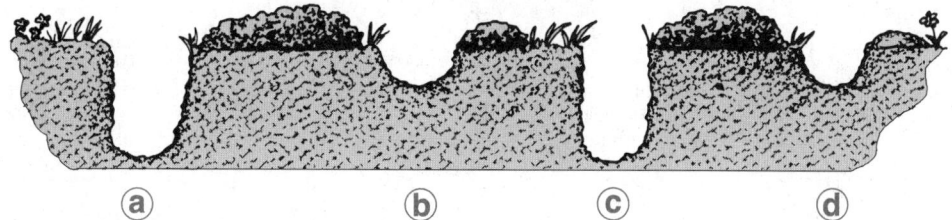

ⓐ   ⓑ   ⓒ   ⓓ

1. Meg did not dig object A. _____

2. Meg dug object C. _____

3. Meg dug object D. _____

D

A lion is to carnivorous as a gorilla is to _____.

herbivorous
canine
amphibian

A

1. deep, lucky, smooth	objects	actions	tell what kind
2. elephant, dish, train	objects	actions	tell what kind
3. masticate, instruct, comprehend	objects	actions	tell what kind
4. television, fireplace, airplane	objects	actions	tell what kind
5. wall, bucket, goat	objects	actions	tell what kind

B Write **true, false,** or **maybe.**

> **Here's the only thing Nan did.**
> **Nan dropped some small cups.**

ⓐ ⓑ ⓒ ⓓ

1. Nan dropped object B. _____

2. Nan dropped object A. _____

3. Nan dropped object C. _____

TEST 5

A

		objects	actions	tell what kind
1. shiny, long, fat		objects	actions	tell what kind
2. flower, canine, bike		objects	actions	tell what kind
3. blanket, street, purse		objects	actions	tell what kind
4. modify, run, sew		objects	actions	tell what kind
5. dull, indolent, striped		objects	actions	tell what kind

B Underline the carnivorous animals.
Circle the herbivorous animals.

C

ⓐ ⓑ ⓒ ⓓ

1. _____
2. _____
3. _____

D

 ①  ②  ③  ④ ⑤

R	R	R	R	R
T	X	T	T	X
M	A	M	A	M
C	B	B	C	C

1. Pass   Fail   **2.** Pass   Fail   **3.** Pass   Fail

E   **1.** Pass   Fail   **2.** Pass   Fail   **3.** Pass   Fail

A

B

C

1. _____
2. _____
3. _____
4. _____

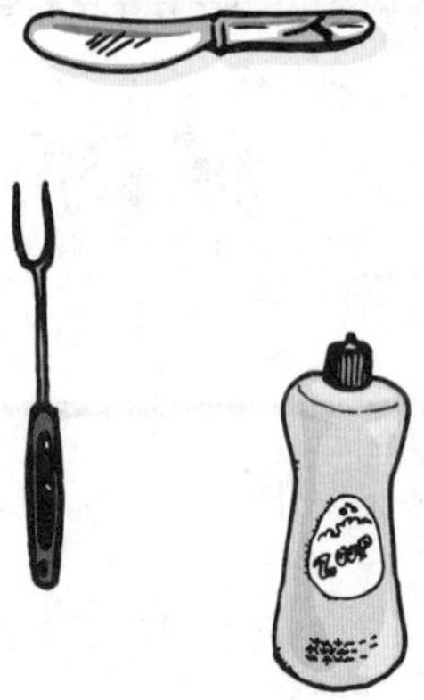

ⓒ   ⓓ   ⓔ

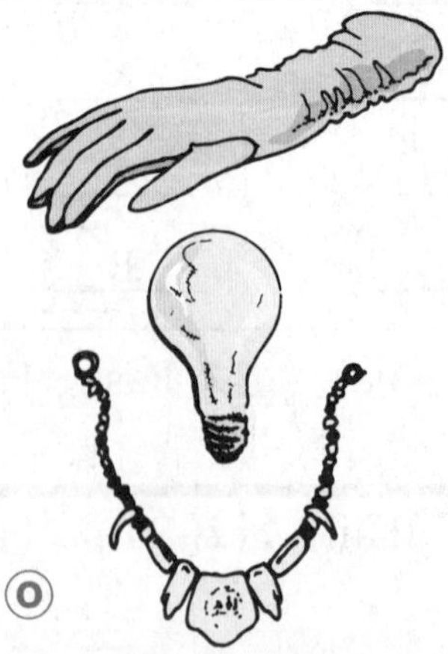

D

1. _____
2. _____
3. _____
4. _____

ⓜ   ⓝ   ⓞ

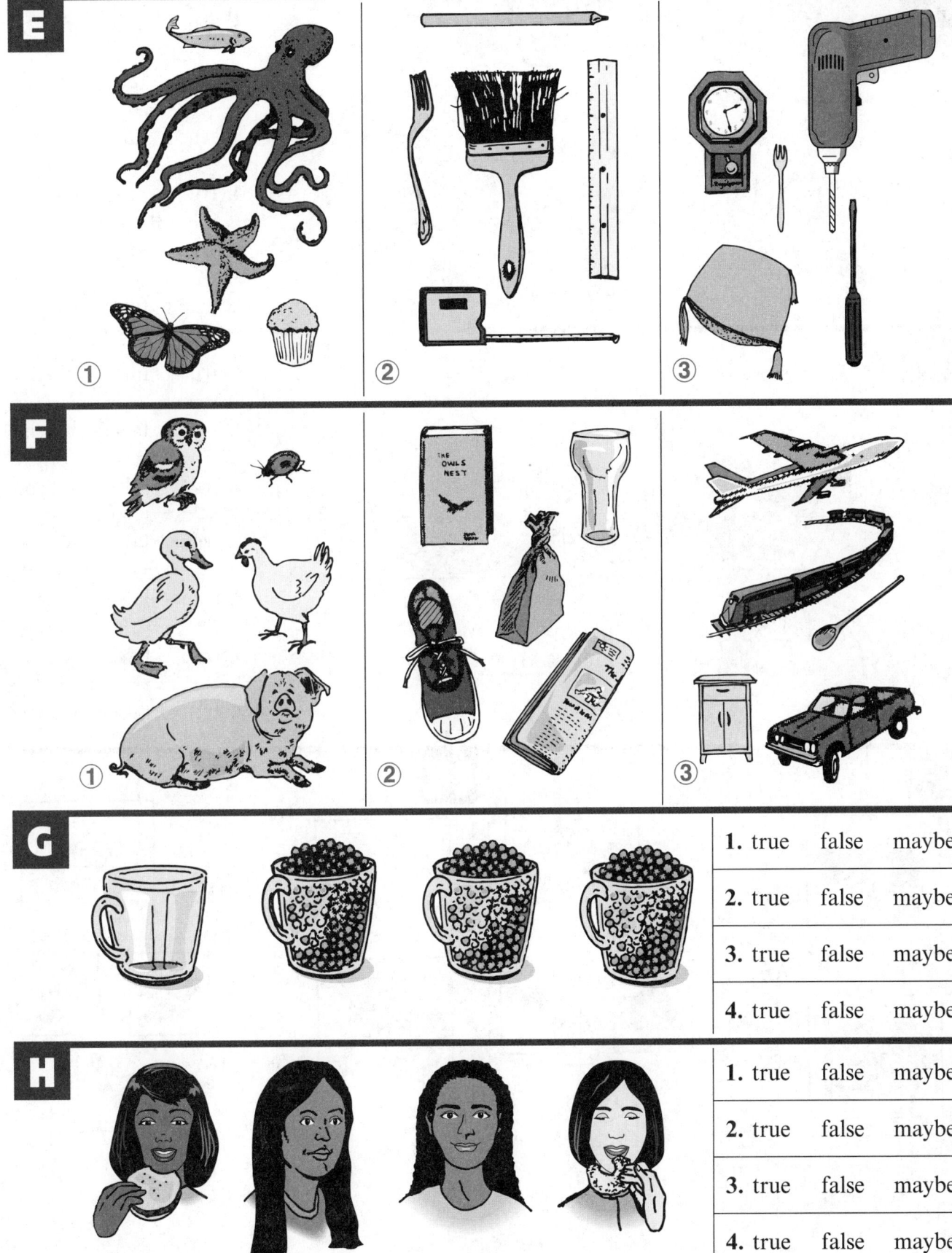

E

① ② ③

F

① ② ③

G

1. true   false   maybe
2. true   false   maybe
3. true   false   maybe
4. true   false   maybe

H

1. true   false   maybe
2. true   false   maybe
3. true   false   maybe
4. true   false   maybe

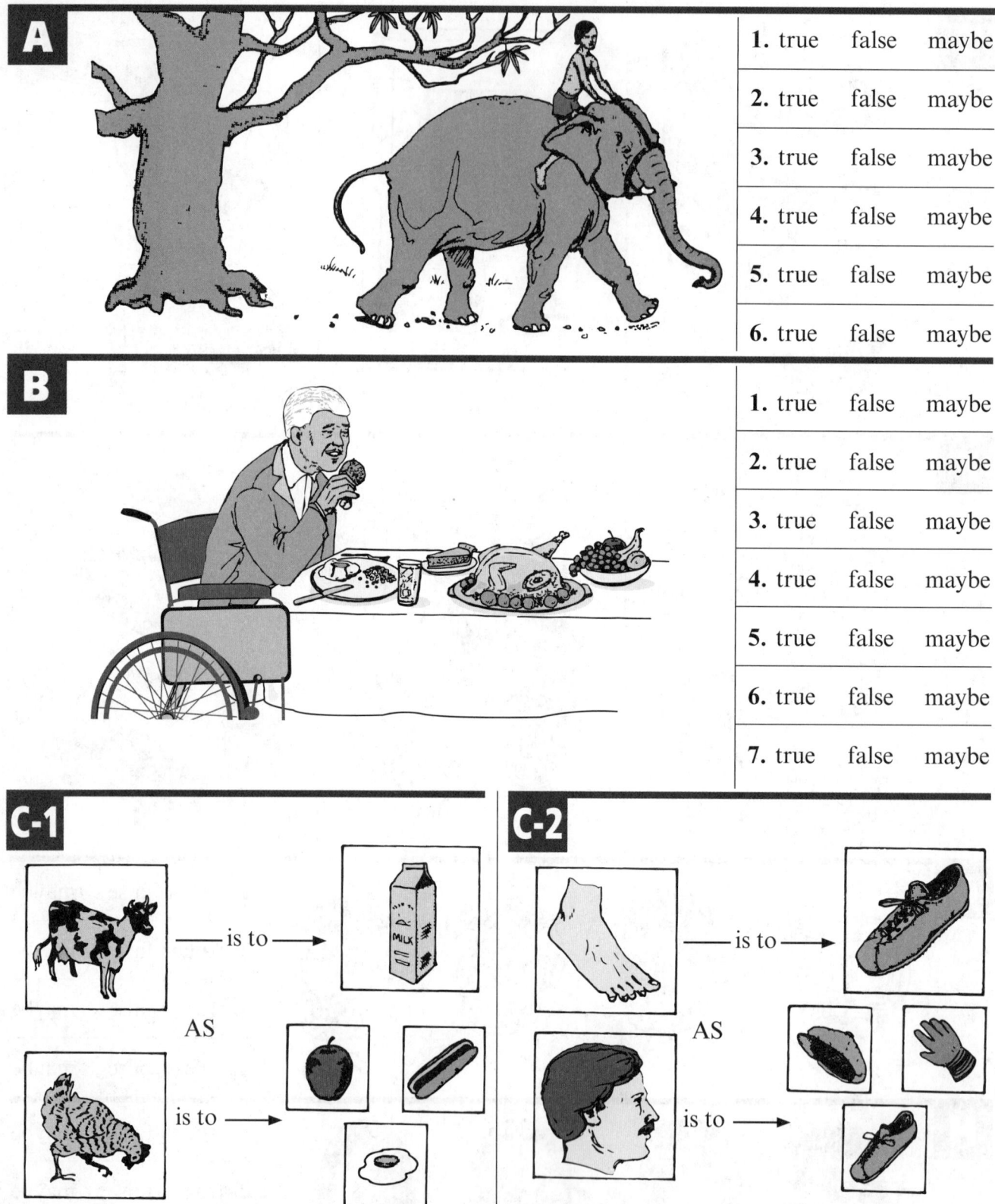

A

1. true   false   maybe
2. true   false   maybe
3. true   false   maybe
4. true   false   maybe
5. true   false   maybe
6. true   false   maybe

B

1. true   false   maybe
2. true   false   maybe
3. true   false   maybe
4. true   false   maybe
5. true   false   maybe
6. true   false   maybe
7. true   false   maybe

C-1

is to

AS

is to

C-2

is to

AS

is to

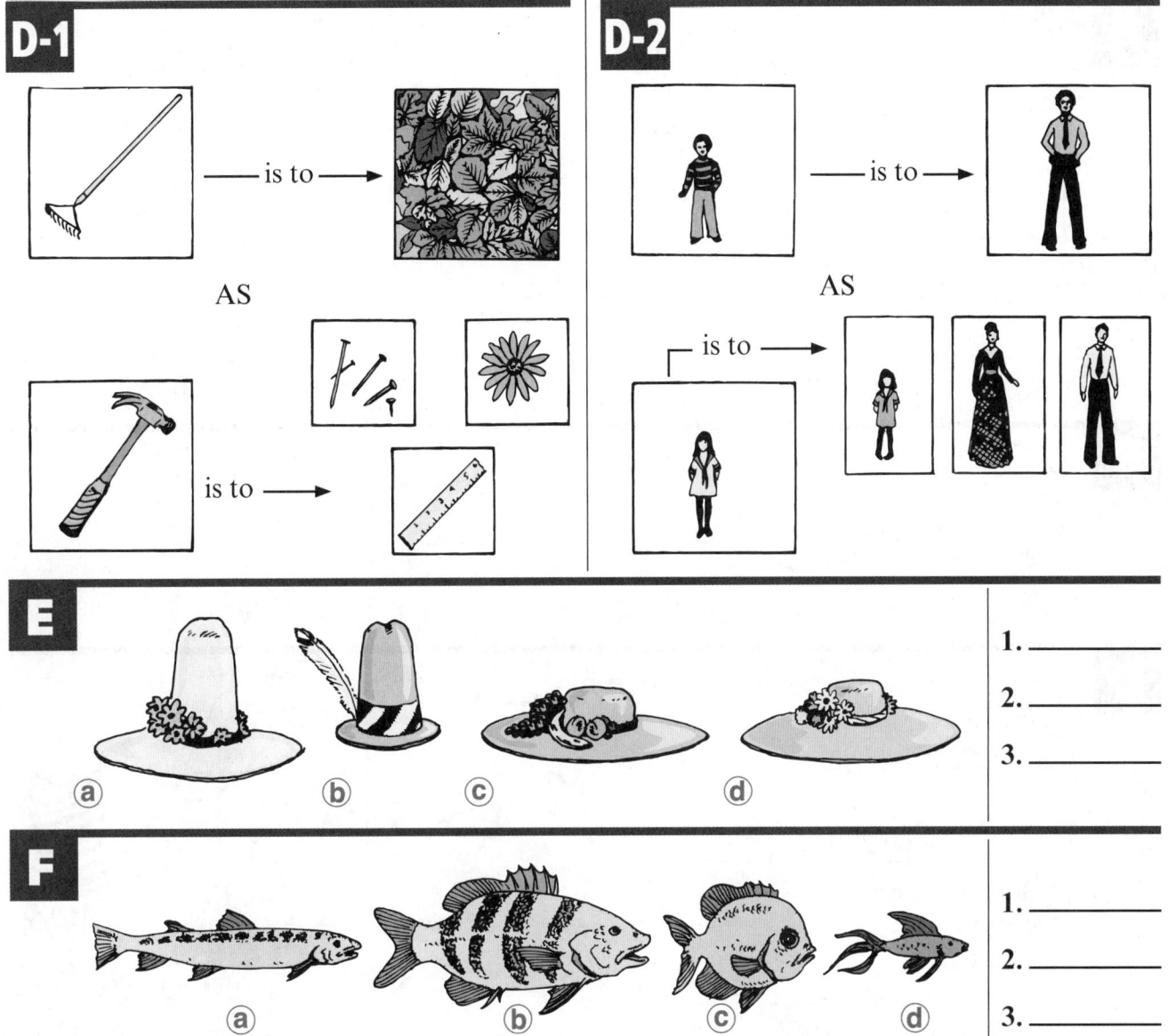

D-1

D-2

E

1. _____
2. _____
3. _____

F

1. _____
2. _____
3. _____

A

① ② ③ ④ ⑤

B

① ② ③ ④ ⑤

C

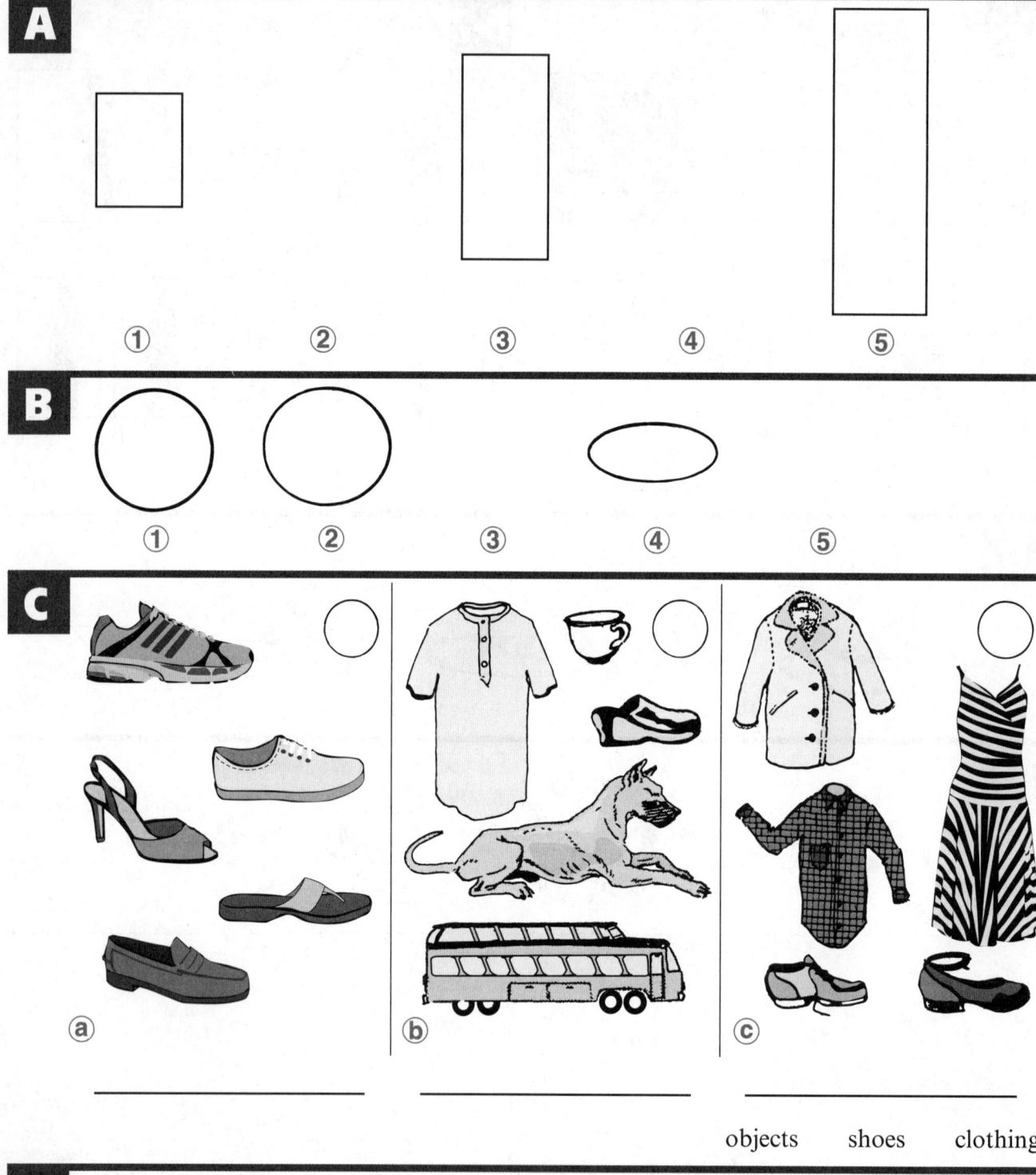

ⓐ ⓑ ⓒ

objects   shoes   clothing

D

A pencil is to wood as a nail is to _____.

metal
plastic
paper

E

Grass is to short as a tree is to _____.

fat
tall
short

F

(a) _____

(b) _____

(c)

containers   cups   objects

G

Here's the only thing we know about Tom. Tom did not write with the fat pencils.

(a)   (b)   (c)   (d)

1. Tom wrote with object A. _____

2. Tom wrote with object B. _____

3. Tom wrote with object C. _____

H

Here's the only thing we know about Jane. Jane did not swing the black bats.

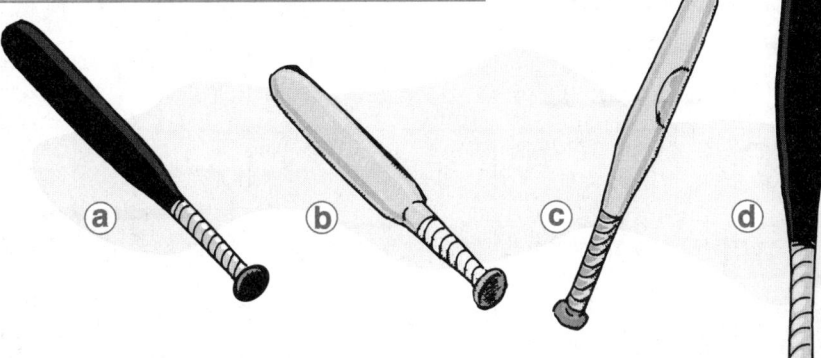

(a)   (b)   (c)   (d)

1. Jane swung object D. _____

2. Jane swung object C. _____

3. Jane swung object B. _____

A

	objects	actions
1. reading, wearing a coat, descend, go	objects	actions
2. drinking coffee, pull, fall, seeing	objects	actions
3. coffee, bus, coats, airplane, sharks	objects	actions
4. talking, duplicate, sipping a milkshake	objects	actions
5. popcorn, milkshake, notebook, canine	objects	actions

B

	objects	actions
1. telephone, dress, car, butterfly, bus	objects	actions
2. talking on a telephone, eating, riding	objects	actions
3. skated, sit, breathe	objects	actions
4. stand up, clean, paddle	objects	actions
5. machine, wagon, cat, pencil, chair	objects	actions

C

D

1. When the moon was half full, a tiger roared.
2. When the moon was half full, a tiger chased a butterfly.
3. When the moon was half full, a tiger drank from a river.

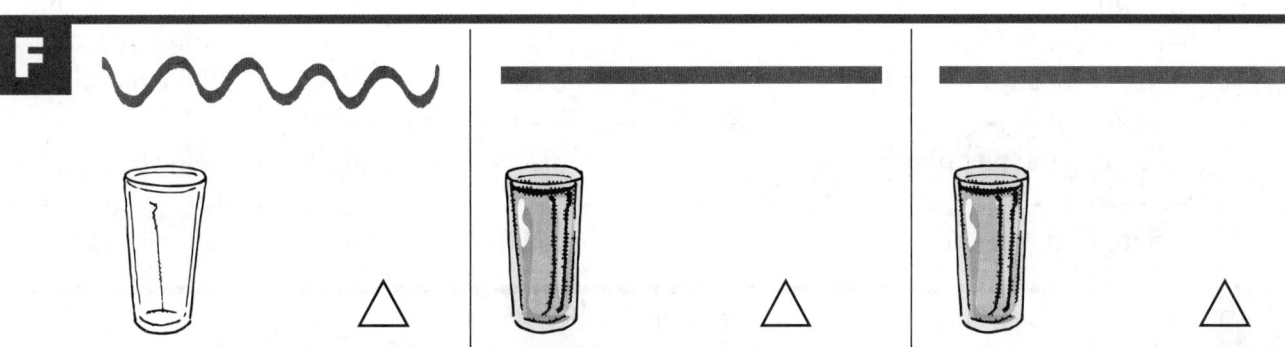

1. When the line is wavy, the glass is full.
2. When the line is straight,the glass is empty.
3. When the line is straight, the glass is full.

Test 5 Review (Lesson 60)

A

1. obtain, duplicate, examine	objects	actions	tell what kind
2. large, funny, wild	objects	actions	tell what kind
3. comprehend, exhibit, inquire	objects	actions	tell what kind
4. shiny, dull, striped	objects	actions	tell what kind
5. construct, consume, complete	objects	actions	tell what kind

B

1. vehicles, appliance, animal	objects	actions	tell what kind
2. pitcher, stove, bread	objects	actions	tell what kind
3. climb, shout, spell	objects	actions	tell what kind
4. thin, purple, plastic	objects	actions	tell what kind
5. real, hard, soft	objects	actions	tell what kind

C
Make a box around the herbivorous animals.
Circle the carnivorous animals.

D
Make a **C** on the carnivorous animals.
Make an **H** on the herbivorous animals.

102   *Review for Test 5*

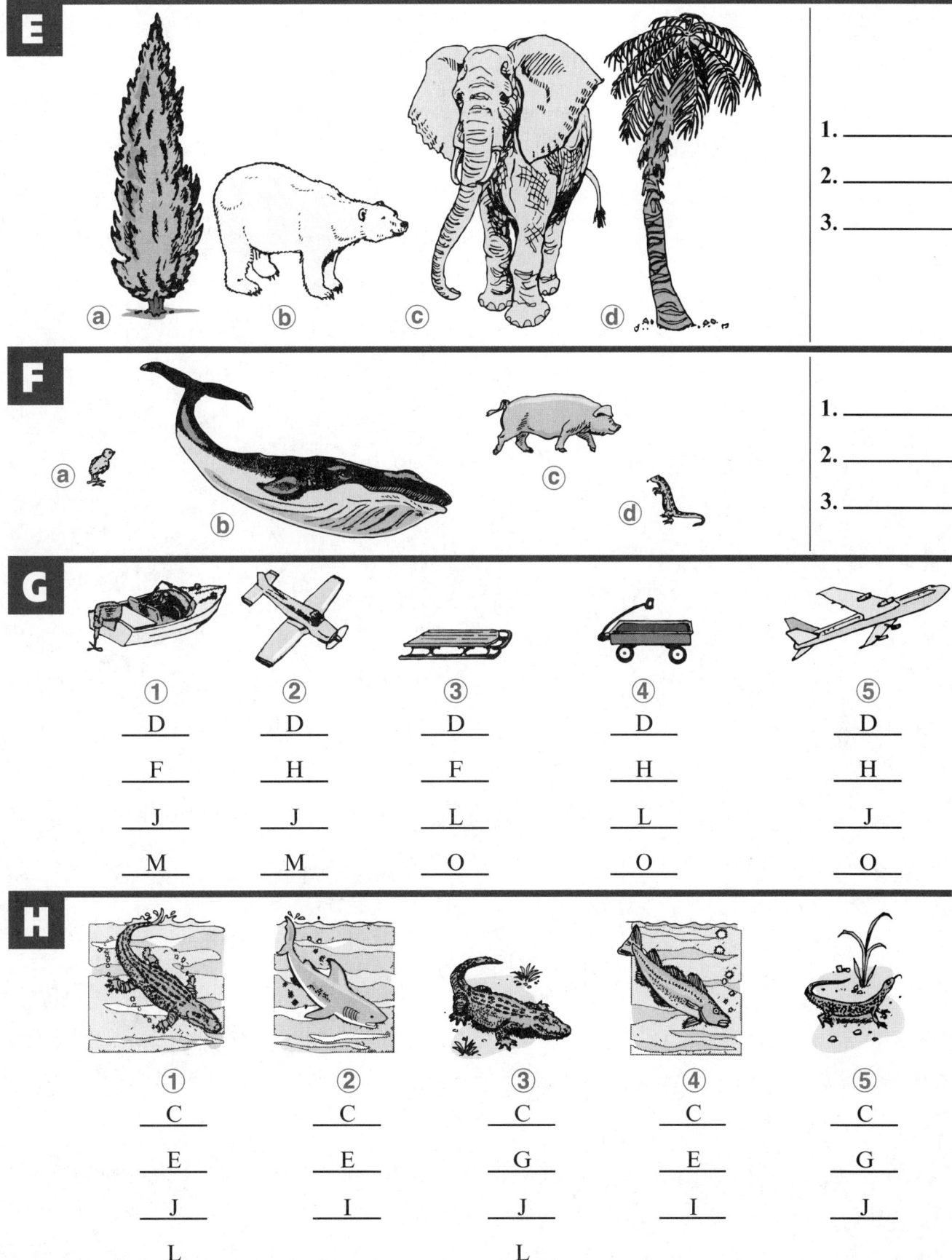

E

a   b   c   d

1. _____
2. _____
3. _____

F

a   b   c   d

1. _____
2. _____
3. _____

G

①	②	③	④	⑤
D	D	D	D	D
F	H	F	H	H
J	J	L	L	J
M	M	O	O	O

H

①	②	③	④	⑤
C	C	C	C	C
E	E	G	E	G
J	I	J	I	J
L	L